3 —

A GUIDE TO
THE CITY OF GOD

A GUIDE TO
THE CITY OF GOD

by

MARTHINUS VERSFELD

SHEED & WARD · NEW YORK

FIRST PUBLISHED 1958
BY SHEED AND WARD LTD
33 MAIDEN LANE
LONDON W.C.2
AND
SHEED AND WARD INC.
840 BROADWAY
NEW YORK 3

Library of Congress Catalog Card Number 58-10556

NIHIL OBSTAT:
> JOANNES M. T. BARTON, S.T.D., L.S.S.
>> *Censor Deputatus*

IMPRIMATUR:
> E. MORROGH BERNARD
>> *Vicarius Generalis*

Westmonasterii, die 27a Januarii, 1958

Manufactured in the United States of America

Magnum quemdam virum et vere humanissimum praedicas.

St. Augustine, *De Musica.*

CONTENTS

INTRODUCTION

THE book before you is a kind of guide-book to St. Augustine's *City of God*, and I ought to tell you why and how it has been written.

For some years I have lectured to university students on the *De Civitate Dei*, and have always found the course a success. Augustine opens a vast and rich world to the mind, and when properly presented links up in a vital way with contemporary life and experience. What he supplies is a total view which seems to appeal to minds starved of means towards synthetic interpretation. Again, the personal nature of his writings makes immediate contact.

The reason why I originally introduced the study of Augustine was that while every student of moral philosophy finished his course with some knowledge of the Greek philosophers, he knew very little of the Hebreo-Christian tradition. Open nearly any well-known textbook on ethics and observe the lacuna. And yet the latter tradition is the more important. What we have is a bias in our universities against the past of our own civilization. Augustine has done more for the formation of the West than Plato, though translations of and commentaries on Plato are legion. Augustine is an excellent introduction to a biblical way of thinking, besides having been so excellent a bearer of classical thought into our own history that it has worked to his detriment.

In no work of his is Augustine more fully presented than in the *City of God*. It contains nearly his whole mind, and what I have striven to do is to bring out the mind of Augustine. This may seem presumptuous, but experience has shown me that students confronted with the book get lost in the thickets. They need a guide to explain the architecture, to isolate the leading principles and to indicate the line and coherence of the argument. On the other hand, no guide-book is a substitute for the text. I have tried to stimulate to the reading of the text by following it chapter after chapter yet in a way which will, I trust, not make this book entirely unreadable by itself.

It will very soon be noticed that I am a philosopher and not a theologian or a classical scholar or a historian. That has its advantages and its disadvantages. At any rate it opens a slant on Augustine which fills a gap among the current works in the English tongue. I am very grateful to recent writers like R. H. Barrow and J. H. S. Burleigh who supply many of my deficiencies, and greatly assist the student. If I criticize Barrow it is because I often use his book. I can't say fairer.

I have dealt only with the last twelve books. The student who has grasped their construction will know how to deal with the first ten. The converse is not true. What is aimed at is a guide, an *apéritif*, not an exhaustive commentary.

A PLAN OF STUDY

THE study of St. Augustine requires some knowledge of his life and times. The best approach to him is through the *Confessions*.

The Confessions of St. Augustine, tr. by F. Sheed, London, 1943.

O'MEARA, J. J., *The Young Augustine*, London, 1954.

There are many books which deal with Augustine in relation to his times. We can mention here:

D'ARCY, M. C., S.J., and others, *A Monument to St. Augustine*, London 1930 (ch. i, "St. Augustine and His Age", by Christopher Dawson.)

MARROU, H. I., *S. Augustin et la fin de la culture antique*, Paris, 1938.

General surveys of Augustine's thought which are easily available are:

GILSON, E., *Introduction à l'étude de S. Augustin*, Paris, 1929. (Excellent bibliography).

COPLESTON, F., *A History of Philosophy*, London, 1950, vol. ii.

Coming now to the *City of God* itself, there is a translation easily obtainable:

The City of God, tr. Healey, ed. R. V. G. Tasker, Everyman's Library Edition, London, 1945. (Latin text ed. J. E. C. Welldon, London, S.P.C.K., 1924.)

Books about the *City of God* are fairly numerous. Two recent studies in English are:

BARROW, R. H., *Introduction to St. Augustine*, London, 1950. (Selections, translation and commentary).

BURLEIGH, J. H. S., *The City of God*, London, 1949.

Readers particularly interested in the political aspects should consult:

FIGGIS, J. N., *The Political Aspects of St. Augustine's City of God*, London, 1921.

COMBÈS, G., *La Doctrine politique de S. Augustin*, Paris, 1927.

Those who desire a survey of Augustine's moral doctrine will find it done briefly and well in

ROLAND-GOSSELIN, B., *La Morale de S. Augustin*, Paris, 1925.

It is invidious to select among so much that is good, however. Not everybody has access to the right kind of library, and one should recommend what there is some chance of obtaining from the booksellers. It should be added that nothing is more indispensable for studying St. Augustine than the Scriptures. Reading St. Augustine presupposes some knowledge of the Christian faith, and what he considered that to be will be found in his own summary, the *Enchiridion*, of which there is an English translation (*The Works of Aurelius Augustine*, ed. M. Dods, Edinburgh, 1873, vol. ix).

How one tackles the subject is a matter of taste. It is best to start with Augustine himself and build out from that. The *Confessions* has the greatest intrinsic attraction. It cannot be denied that the *City of God* is somewhat forbidding, and in a first reading the first ten books could well be omitted.

I

ST. AUGUSTINE AND *THE CITY OF GOD*

Sᴛ. Augustine (354-430) is one of the great bridges between classical antiquity and the modern world. He brought together what was living in the intellectual and spiritual life of his time in a synthesis which did an incalculable amount to shape the minds and institutions of the subsequent centuries.

He stands out as a great and vital personality. He is great as a man. We know a great deal about his life because his autobiography, the *Confessions*, is perhaps the most famous of all autobiographies.

In spite of the enormous bulk of his written works Augustine was not primarily a student or a man of letters but a Christian bishop, a busy administrator, priest and preacher. His writings cover a considerable range, and include a work on music, but the best-known are the *Confessions*, the *De Civitate Dei* and the *De Trinitate*. Much of his life was given to the defence of the Church against the Manichees, the Donatists and the Pelagians, against whom he wrote treatises. These are also commentaries on the Scriptures, a great series of sermons on the Psalms, handbooks on Christian doctrine, and so on. Thus Augustine was much more than merely a philosopher. He was vitally concerned with theology, doctrine, morals and politics—thus, with all the great motives that control human conduct.

Augustine was an African, what nowadays we should call an Algerian, born at Tagaste in A.D. 354, when Africa was a Roman province. His mother Monnica was a Christian, his father, Patricius, a pagan, one of the small landed gentry. As a small boy he was quick, vital, warm-hearted and very fond of games, especially games of skill and chance. He received a thorough classical education at Madaura, from whence dates his fondness for Vergil, and then went on with higher studies in the gay licentious seaport atmosphere of Carthage. He was a brilliant student of rhetoric, fond of sexual and other pleasures, and with a considerable gift for friendships. Though brought up as a Christian by Monnica he accepted and propagated the Manichean heresy in Carthage because he thought it gave an explanation of the problem of evil.

From Carthage he went to Rome, ambitious to make his name in the capital. We must remember that by that time the official religion of the Roman Empire was Christianity, though this was still bitterly opposed by many pagans in the name of the great traditions of ancient Rome. From Rome he went to Milan to an official post as rhetor, made the acquaintance of the great Bishop Ambrose, and underwent the stirring conversion to the Christian faith described in the *Confessions*, having first abandoned Manicheism for neo-Platonism. After a period of retirement in which he made his reckoning with some of the sceptical trends in contemporary philosophy, he returned to Africa, founded a monastic community, was elected Bishop of Hippo, and was involved in pastoral cares, and—often in danger of assassination—in the Donatist controversy.

He lived in the thunder of the downfall of the Roman Empire. Alaric and the Goths sacked the City in 410, and when Augustine died in 430 the Vandals were breaking into Hippo. One may say that his life-work was to kindle the light of things eternal in human hearts no longer supported by temporal institutions which had seemed eternal but which were crashing on all sides.

Perhaps more than any other man Augustine was knitting together the enduring elements in a disintegrating civilization, and making them fruitful for the subsequent centuries. In Rome two great streams had met: the Graeco-Roman literary and philosophic tradition, and, from Palestine, the Judaeo-Christian revelation. Platonism, Epicureanism and Stoicism had come to Rome, where Cicero and Vergil wrote, and so had the apostles Peter and Paul. The Christians had been persecuted and superficially there had seemed to be an irreconcilability between the achievements of Greece and Rome, and the religion revealed in Palestine. So it appeared from both sides. The cultivated pagan regarded the Christians as uncouth and subversive; the Christian often regarded the literature and philosophy of Greece and Rome as merely human vanities. But in fact the philosophy required a new substance to express, while the new faith sought to find expression in new languages and through new ways of elaboration. The quarrel continues to the present day, but the future lay with men who could harmonize the best in the pagan intellect with their Christian faith, and of these Augustine was the greatest.

We have mentioned that in the interval between his rejection of the Manichees and his conversion, Augustine was a Platonist. Plato and neo-Platonism were the chief formatives of Augustine's mind on the philosophic side. Students approaching Augustine from the study of Plato will recognize the extent of the debt, but it would be a mistake to recognize mainly the Greek element in St. Augustine. He was primarily a Christian bishop and not a philosopher, and he is much more influenced by the Church and the Scriptures than by the schools and the philosophies. It is to revelation rather than to rational speculation that he looks for truth, and it is through history rather than through metaphysics that he seeks to discern the ways of God.

If we want to find the whole man in the widest scope of his interests and powers we shall find him in the *City of God*. Here we find Augustine as theologian, as philosopher, as moralist, as political thinker, as interpreter of history, as literary and dramatic censor, as critic of his times and as apologist. In spite of the differences, it is worth noticing the resemblances in aim and scope between the *Republic* and *Laws* of Plato, and the *City of God* of St. Augustine. The situations of the two men were not entirely dissimilar. Plato had seen the rending of Greece by the Peloponnesian War, and had endeavoured to deal with the spiritual situation which underlay it. He achieved a vision of social life as resting on righteousness, he grasped the essential interdependence and social character of men and the primacy of the true and the good in social relationships, and he rose to a conception of a justice which is not a convention of man but an eternal prescription written in the nature of things. He described a city which can never be fully realized on earth, but in which the just man can participate through the immortal element in himself, and in the course of his description he saw profoundly how theology, philosophy, politics, art, morals and science cohere and influence each other in the unity of the human good. Augustine too is writing of no earthly city, but of a society where men shall enjoy an eternal blessedness which no temporal community can give. Like Plato he contrasts the city of the unjust with the city of the just, and for both men our righteousness or unrighteousness determines our condition after death.

We should be wrong, however, if we saw the resemblances only at the cost of the differences. The *Republic* is a construction of human philosophical thought. It is an attempt to say how men would live if the implications of their rationality were to be worked out. There is nothing in fact corresponding to it, and it could come into being only by the chance of a philosopher's becoming a king or a king's becoming a philosopher. In that sense it is an ideal construction, a project, something that exists only in words. Look at the conclusion of *Repub.*, ix:

> I understand, he said. You speak of the city whose foundation we have been describing, which has its being in words, for there is no spot on earth, I imagine, where it exists.

No, I said, but perhaps it is laid up in heaven as a pattern for him who wills to see, and seeing, to found a city in himself. Whether it exists anywhere or ever will exist, is no matter.

But while on the one hand existence is indifferent to it, on the other it is affected—one might say, tainted—throughout with the conditions of historical existence. For instance, its realization is contingent and its decline is inevitable. Its inhabitants know sickness and war. Doctors, judges and soldiers will find material for the exercise of their professions. Those guardians most trained to despise the body and bodily feelings must propagate most. The ruler, in taking up his office, is returning to the cares of the world. Even this ideal city is no abiding commonwealth, and its perfection is only relative to existing conditions. Further, it is not a city into which we enter through death, by the divine grace and by the divine judgement.

Here we come to one aspect of the puzzles about the connections between Plato's philosophy and his religion and eschatology. The *Republic*, like the *Gorgias*, concludes with a tale of a judgement after death. Those who have preferred righteousness to unrighteousness will pass to felicity after judgement by a divine judge. The rewards of the just life in the just city "are nothing in number or greatness compared with those which await each man after death". The just man passes then to a greater friendship with himself and with the gods, and to membership of a community superior to that of the philosophers' Republic, by living according to the rules of which, however, he merits the rewards of the after-life.

We have then in Plato two supra-terrestrial communities, one existing in the words of philosophers and still tainted with the necessities of human life, and the other existing as a religious fact describable only in terms of myth.

I leave out the cyclical elements in Plato's position, important though they are, and proceed at once to point out a difference between the positions of Plato and Augustine. For Augustine there is no philosophers' city floating like Mahomet's coffin between the actualities of history and the community of the blessed spirits. Augustine, with his scriptural background, is much more realistic and positive in his attitude to history. We are not to embark upon a dialectic which detaches us from the actual, but to discuss the spiritual forces which are and have been actually at work in the history of the human race. Our endeavour is to come to terms with what is rather than to shelter from the hail and dust in a city which has its being in words. Augustine is more concerned to describe this vale of tears, and to fortify us for our life in it, than to excogitate ideal types for an ideal environment. He is more historically minded. Admirable as the wise empiricism of Republic VIII and IX is, we are still confronted with a process of typification, with the construction—as in Thucydides—of a diagram which will fit events as long as human nature remains what it is. Augustine has a stronger sense of the linear character of history, and of the uniqueness of historical events. Both are looking for a meaning, but whereas Plato finds it by relating an event to a type, Augustine finds an immanent meaning in events themselves. It is this "type-thinking" which leads to the conception of a circularity of occurrences. In brief, the Utopian element is absent in Augustine.

But as Augustine's grip on historical fact is stronger, so is his grip on religion. The *Civitas Dei* is neither an ideal, nor is it something which can be described only in terms of myth. It is an actually existing community of which we have not philosophic nor imaginative knowledge, but the certainty of revealed truth. We are certain that God created it, that it exists; and we know a good deal about it from the Scriptures. Consequently we are more certain in our orientations to it. Augustine presents it to us as a massive certainty, above the fluctuations of speculation or imagination; as a fact to which we have access because God has made it possible. To the degree that we come to terms

with it, our Utopias can look after themselves. It is not that with
which we end our treatise on the City but that with which we
start it. Hence the opening words of the *De Civitate Dei* are:
"That most glorious society and celestial city of God's faithful".

Augustine thus makes it clear from the commencement that
he is founding his treatise on Scripture. "We give the name of
the City of God unto that society whereof that Scripture bears
witness ... For there it is said: Glorious things are spoken of
thee, thou City of God." These words occur at the beginning
of Book XI, that is, at the opening of the second half of the
De Civitate Dei, and like the opening words of it they refer to
Psalm LXXXVI. The city of which he is speaking is the
heavenly Jerusalem, the city of peace, to which all nations are
called by the divine election. The "Gates of Sion" have been
opened by Christ to all the nations and He will gather them,
together into the city of His peace. We can see a development
throughout the Old Testament from a nationalistic religion to the
conception of Yahweh as the God of all men and the Judge of
all nations. This universalism reaches one of its highest Old
Testament expressions in Psalm LXXXVI. On it Augustine
comments: "In this psalm the praises of a certain city are sung;
we are resident aliens in it as long as we are in this life; to it we
press on, but the way to it is barred ... and could not be found
till the King of the city made Himself the way." We pass then
from a Jerusalem which is the political and religious capital of
the Jews, to a city of which Christ is the King. We arrive there
not by the dialectic of philosophers but through the providential
governance of history by God, a redemptive process in which
we are all actively implicated, and whose relevance to the affairs
of Rome Augustine is prepared to exhibit. The references to
Rome in I, 1 are clear, where Augustine turns the words of their
own poet, Vergil, against the Romans, quoting the words,

Parcere subjectis, et debellare superbos

to suggest that Rome is not heavenly and eternal but terrene, and has been punished by God for *superbia*.

The occasion for the composition of the *De Civitate Dei* was the capture of Rome by the Goths in A.D. 410 and it may be regarded as an attempt to reorientate minds, both pagan and Christian, which had been shattered by the fall of a city which had seemed eternal. Even a man like Jerome had been hard hit by the news. It made necessary a rethinking of attitudes to things temporal, and to the part played in our lives by a temporal polity. But primarily the work was polemically undertaken. It was written *contra paganos*. Rome was officially Christian. But many Romans, and some in high places, were pagans. To the latter it seemed that the fall of Rome had a religious explanation. The pagan deities were the true gods taking vengeance on Rome for its apostasy. Could Christian apologetics meet the grave accusation that it was Christianity which had broken the old Roman fibre? This was the challenge which Augustine took up. He undertook to show that it was the irreligion and immorality of Rome which was the true cause of her downfall, to exhibit the character of all earthly societies, to show men that the City of God alone was eternal, and to demonstrate that Rome had become pre-eminent only insofar as she had displayed virtues pleasing to the true God.

The more negative and polemical side of Augustine's undertaking is carried out in books i-x. "In these ten books I have spoken, by the good assistance of God ... against the impious contradictors that prefer their gods before the Founder of the holy city whereof we are to dispute. The first five of the ten opposed them that adored their gods for temporal respects: the five latter were against those that adored them for the life to come." "We deal not against atheists, nor such as exclude the gods from dealing in man's affairs, but with such as prefer their gods before our God, the Founder of this glorious city."

If we call the first ten books the more negative and polemical, this must be taken in a rough and relative way. There is a good deal that is polemical in the later books, and much of Augustine's positive doctrine in the earlier. For instance, his treatment of human suffering in times of war, and his arguments on suicide in Book I, are of lasting value. In reading the later books we can constantly go back to the earlier for supplementation. Nevertheless it is idle to pretend that the earlier books are not of lesser interest to the present-day reader. Many of the controversies raised are as dead as these things ever become, and there is a good deal to be said for reading the *De Civitate Dei* selectively. Augustine worked at it for fifteen years and some of it may be taken to be occasional writing. It should be remembered, however, that much of the boredom arising from the earlier books is due to lack of historical imagination, and disappears if we try to reconstruct Augustine in his surroundings. Plato was right when he said that man was the State writ small, and Augustine has the advantage of realizing this dictum in a more vivid and historical way. What he gives us in the *Confessions* is primarily the history of his soul, but the macrocosm which this history reflects is the history of the Roman Empire. In the *City of God* we see the outer drama in which the inner drama was involved. St. Augustine's conversion was the conversion of a culture, and the first ten books go far to give an empirical content to this statement.

Augustine was converted not only from his own sins but from the whole world and culture in which he had found his temptations, and which had condoned his sins; and to understand his life and work we should try to *imagine* the world depicted in the *De Civitate Dei*. Augustine gives us the means to people the pallid phrase "Roman religious practices" with a host of astrologers, magicians, soothsayers, necromancers, stage-players and the like. For instance, he puts us into a position to evoke a world of temple prostitutes and temple sodomites, and is standing close to his own experience when he speaks of the Ganymedes who "against all shame of man and woman, went with anointed heads, painted faces, relaxed bodies and lascivious paces up and down the streets of Carthage." He is referring to the *galli*, the self-castrated votaries of Cybele, and he catches the very echoes of a Carthaginian street when he speaks of the "timbrels, turrets, eunuchs, ravings and cymbals" of the Mother Goddess. To get that is to move from a notional towards a real comprehension of what it meant to him to belong to the Body of Christ. Christ was for Augustine He who had put an end to his own complicity in such a society, and had brought this culture under condemnation.

We shall, however, concentrate here on the later books, endeavouring to bring out the unity and line of the argument, and the scope of its vast conception. I am addressing myself principally to students like those to whom for many years I have had the privilege of speaking about Augustine, and I shall explain the things which I found it necessary to explain to them. The *City of God*, like the *Republic* of Plato, offers a grand opportunity for introducing the reader to the *whole* mind of a great man, and that opportunity should be taken. We can approach it with specialist interests—as theologians, as political philosophers, as historians, as classical scholars, and so on. The most profitable approach for the ordinary educated reader is to try to see the mind of Augustine as it was and to bring out the importance of those things which he thought important. For example, in his edition of the text of the *De Civitate Dei*, Welldon refers to Augustine's doctrine of the eternal punishment of the damned as though it were a quaint old-fashioned quirk which "we" have got beyond.[1] *Bon voyage* to those who think they have, but it was not the mind of St. Augustine. Again, commentators sometimes do not give full weight to Augustine's angelology. But Augustine not only believed in angels but considered their

[1] Introd., pp. xii-xiii.

activity to be of the highest political relevance. We shall try to look objectively at Augustine, and that will be impossible if we are not prepared to enter subjectively into the mind of a man who was primarily a bishop and a theologian.

II

BOOK XI: THE CITY'S FOUNDATION

WE shall endeavour, then, to wend our way through the work from Book XI onwards, remembering that what I am writing is not a substitute for reading St. Augustine but a sort of guide-book which will often be content to say, Go here or there, or, Do this or that.

At the end of Book X Augustine states his programme clearly. "It remains now, according as we promised in the first book, to proceed in our discourse of the two cities that are confused to-gether in this world and distinct in the other; whose origin, pro-gress, and consummation I will now unfold, evermore invoking the assistance of the Almighty."

XI, 1   Augustine tells us that there is a City of God "whereof the Scripture bears witness". The Scriptures "teach us that there is a City of God, whereof His inspired love makes us desire to be members". Likewise, there is a city of those who reject the love of God. Like the wheat and the tares in the parable these two cities lie confusedly together in this world, and Augustine wishes to tell us how they came into being, how they have waxed to-gether in the course of history, and how God will finally separate them at the end of history.

The City of God is the society of those who love God. It is not an ideal city or a Utopia but the living and actual fellowship of those who have responded to the love of God. In his treatise *On Christian Doctrine*, Augustine uses the analogy of the theatre to bring before us the manner in which men can be united by admiration for a person. "In the theatres ... if a man is fond of a particular actor, and enjoys his art as a good or even as the very greatest good, he is fond of all who join with him in admiration of his favourite, not for their own sakes, but the sake of him whom they admire in common; and the more fervent he is in his admiration, the more he works in every way he can to secure new admirers for him, and the more anxious he becomes to show him to others."[1] A set of human relations, transient in the example of the theatre, is set up which is proportioned to a common good which is the object of love. Similarly a set of relations comes into being when, loving God, we love in other people the love with which they love God. The City of God is the organic whole of these relations. We must remember, however, that we can only so love God because He first loves us. "His inspired love makes us desire to be members." We are answering to a call which we can hear only because God Himself has opened our ears to it. "And now as to love," says Augustine, "the greater the measure in which it dwells in a man, the better is the man in whom it dwells. For when there is a question as to whether a man is good, one does not ask what he believes, or what he hopes, but what he loves."[2] Since this love is inspired, breathed in, by God, the City of God is a community created not by man but by God.

Of this city, then, Augustine undertakes to speak. But what [XI, 2, 3] method is he to employ? Augustine holds that we can know things in different ways and by different capacities. Things like colour, sound and smell we know by the senses. There are non-sensible things, like mathematical truths and moral principles, which we know by the intelligence. Further, there are a number of things which we have to credit on due authority. For instance, we take it on authority that we were born of certain parents, at a certain time and place, or that a certain city exists which in fact we have never seen. In the instances mentioned we credit certain facts by a natural faith. But there are some things which

i, 29.   [2] *Enchiridion*, cvii.

we credit on the authority of God who reveals them to us, and who gives us the faith by which we credit them. Higher than any rational knowledge is revealed truth believed in faith, and given us by the Prophets, by Christ, by the Apostles and by canonical Scripture. Augustine says that the Churches must establish which Scriptures are canonical,[1] and declares: *Ego vero evangelio non crederem nisi me catholicae ecclesiae commoveret auctoritas*[2] —"I should not believe the Gospels themselves did not the authority of the Catholic Church move me thereto."

In speaking of the City of God we have, like philosophers, to employ reason and understanding, but primarily we must invoke God's help and base our words on the truths credited on divine authority. In saying this Augustine intends no depreciation of reason. Reason is an organ of truth, and therefore God-given, the best part of a man. Faith requires of us no diminution of this faculty but rather its enlargement and purification, by giving it higher objects and by removing the moral impediments to its honest employment. Truth is the fruit of humility. Thus Augustine writes to Dioscorus: "To grasp the truth one must above all have a holy submission to God who has seen the uncertainty of our steps, and has Himself marked our paths. The first is humility, the second is humility, and the third is humility." We must believe if we wish really to understand.

XI, 4 ff. At the beginning of Chapter 4 we have a good example of this method.

> Of things visible, the world is the greatest: of invisible, God. But the first we see, the second we but believe. That God made the world, whom shall we believe with more safety than Himself? Where have we heard Him? Never better than in the Holy Scriptures, where the prophet says: "In the beginning God created heaven and earth."

[1] *De Doctr. Chr.*, viii.
[2] *Contra Epist. Fund.*, v. In this book I shall not elaborate on what he meant by *catholica*. But owing to his frequent references to Holy Scripture, it is easy to be deceived about his attitude to ecclesiastical authority, which question is raised in the Donatist controversy rather than in the *De Civitate Dei*.

Augustine is asking us to believe that our world is a created world, and to believe it on the authority of God Himself. He does not first attempt a philosophical demonstration of God's existence, nor advance creation as a speculative hypothesis. His approach is Hebrew, not Greek. Almost immediately he plunges into arguments about space, time and origin, arguments made possible only by his training in Hellenic philosophy. He is reasoning under the attraction of an object given as a thing believed, and the synthesis between Athens and Jerusalem which was to play so large a part in the future formation of the West is well under way.

The notion of creation *ex nihilo* is thinkable as a philosophical hypothesis, but in fact philosophy received it from the Old Testament. It is of quite radical importance for Augustine's thought. It liberated him from the dualism remaining from his Manichean and Platonist periods. God is regarded as the sole Creator, without intermediaries, of the universe. We no longer have a God, or gods, confronted with an alien matter which he must combat, subdue or inform, and which lies behind the universe as an abyss which never ceases to be an actual or possible source of irrationalities in the universe. The menace of irrational chance is lifted. God is absolutely the Creator of whatever is, and there is nothing in anything which it did not receive from God.

Further, God is under no necessity to create. He is not confronted with any challenge outside of Himself, or with any lack or necessity within. God supremely is, the fullness of being. He does not need food, or love, or power, like a man; while were He under any necessity He would be under the command of a power higher than Himself, which is impossible. Why, then, did He create? The only possible answer is: because He is God. Now the Christian God who wholly is, is also wholly love. The Act which is His being is the act which is His Love, and it is in the divine love that we must seek an answer to our question. Let us turn our attention for a moment to human love. At its best it manifests a certain generosity at the core of our being. We wish to give something to someone for the good of the person to whom it is given. The end of sexual love is to be the cause of the good of existence to another being. That is why Augustine holds that polygamy for the sake of children is less sinful than monogamy for the sake of lust. Genuine love of whatever kind seeks an enhancement of being, but human love must be *given* the object whose good it seeks. We are making something of a situation, but we must be given in that situation. Our power to love and the thing loved are both received. Now Augustine holds that an unreceived love, the love of God, requires no received object. It is pure and absolute generosity. And with this generosity goes omnipotence. God in the sheer gratuitousness of His generosity gives the good of being to creatures,[1] not because He seeks or needs anything for Himself, but solely in order that the creature may have the happiness of being drawn to and of receiving the love of God. Creatures owe their being to a superabundance of divine joy which is identical with the divine power and goodness.

It is hardly too much to say that the *De Civitate Dei* is a sustained attempt to draw out the full consequences of this doctrine.

The gratuitousness of creation by and for the love of God is, then, the main point to bear in mind. Augustine was always fascinated by the problems of time,[2] transience and genesis. His mind on these matters is better studied in works like the *Confessions* and the *Commentary on Genesis* than in the *City of God*. He takes time more seriously than any previous thinker, and though we need not go into the details of his explanation of Scripture here, we must draw attention to the opening of XI, 6. Augustine is meeting the question why God chose to create the

---

[1] "Ostendens quam non eis indiguerit, sed eas gratuita bonitate condiderit." (xii, 17.)

[2] "My mind burns to solve this complicated enigma." (*Conf.*, xi, 22.)

world *then* and not at some other time. He sees that the question presupposes a conception of time as an endless vacuity into which created things are arbitrarily interjected. But he makes the reply, so heavy with metaphysical consequences, that time is nothing but the mode of existence of creatures, and that time apart from creatures is quite inconceivable. Time is itself a creature. "For if eternity and time be rightly distinguished, time never to be extant without motion, and eternity to admit no change, who would not see that time could not have being before some movable thing were created, whose motion and successive alteration the time might run by?" Time and history, then, are the expression of the nature and disposition of things willed by God in creating. They are the procession of creatures to the divine love. Time is not an illusion nor the empty receptacle of events but the concrete drama of a created universe. Augustine regards time as an imitation of eternity. In God "there is no time because there is no mutability". How then can things of time imitate God? By their form, order, and harmonious procession. "The things of the earth are subordinated to the things in the heavens, and by the harmonious succession of their times they join the fellowship of the universal poem (*carmini universitatis associant*)". (*De Musica*, vi, ch. xi, 29.)

Augustinian scholars frequently say that Augustine could not XI, 9 plan a book. It is true that he has a burning mind which flares up on all sorts of subjects, but the greater outlines of the *De Civitate Dei* are clear, and the great guiding ideas are firm and profound. Book XI, in spite of its scattered appearance, is a mine of the latter, and its development is clear.

The City takes root in a created universe. It is a community of persons who love God. But Chapter 9 makes clear to us that by persons Augustine did not mean only human persons. A person is a free intelligent being, and Augustine held that there were legions of intelligent beings other than men. The chapter commences: "Now having resolved to relate this holy city's origin, and first of the angels, who make a great part thereof ... let us see what testimonials of Holy Writ concern this point." Augustine holds then that there is a realm of angelic beings, and that angels are the first inhabitants of the *Civitas Dei*. Angels are free, intelligent pure spirits,[1] whose powers of intelligence and action are much greater than those of men.

R. H. Barrow, in his useful *Introduction to St. Augustine*, writes (p. 150): "If, then, evil is to be found at sub-human, human and supra-human levels, its origin must be pushed back to a time prior to the appearance of man on the planet. This is the necessity which the hypothesis of a self-corruption of the angels is intended to meet." Barrow's commentary (pp. 148-52) leaves the reader with the impression that the angels are a hypothesis introduced to deal with the problem of evil. But in the first place the angels are first introduced in Book XI in order to widen our idea of the scope of God's creation and to praise Him in it. Hence the quotation from Psalm CXLVIII which includes the words "Praise Him all ye His angels, praise Him all His hosts." Secondly, no hypothetical postulation is involved. For Augustine the angels were plain matter of fact, vouched for by the Scriptures from Genesis to Revelations. They were messengers and servants of God who stood by the young men in the fiery furnace, announced the Incarnation and the Resurrection, liberated Peter from prison and so on. Their existence might fit certain facts, and this might establish their philosophic probability, but this is not Augustine's approach.

Neither were they for Augustine the rather futile decorative beings of some children's books and some Christmas cards, but beings of immense power who not only play a vital and critical part in human affairs and history, but have an immense world of their own concerns which culminates in the *opus Dei*, the praise of God, which for Augustine is the only proper concern of any intelligent being.

[1] See our remarks on Book XXI, pp. 122-3.

One must mention too that Augustine was not divided from many of his pagan contemporaries on the matter of the existence of pure spirits. The Platonists, neo-Platonists, and gnostics believed in the existence and intervention of *daemones*. The fifth-century treatise of the Pseudo-Denis on the angelic hierarchy is full of these influences, while Plato and the neo-Platonists regarded them as intermediaries in the act of creation, an opinion which Augustine rejects. He does not question the existence of the *daemones* of the philosophers but their beneficence.

For on the authority of the Scriptures Augustine held the existence not only of good angels but of evil angels or devils. A devil is an angel that has gone wrong by the misuse of his freedom. Just as the good angels are the foundation members of the *Civitas Dei*, so the fallen angels are the foundation members of the *civitas terrena*. We can observe from this that *terrena* does not simply mean "of this earth". It means the low or fallen city. There was sin in the heavens before there was sin on earth.

There is then one city of good angels and men, and another city of evil angels and men. What we must reflect upon is that each city is *one*.[1] When we say that a community is one community, we mean that its members have a common end, that each is relevant to each, and that the actions of each affect the actions of all, and vice versa. If men and angels form one city this must hold of that city. The actions of angels must affect the actions of men, and the actions of men those of angels. They exist in co-operation. It is difficult to exaggerate how seriously Augustine takes this conception. He holds that there is not only an extraordinary contact between angels and men, such as the Annunciation, but an ordinary or daily influence. Human history is merely a part of a larger drama moving according to a strategy much clearer to the angelic intelligences than to our own. When he says that the gods of Rome were devils luring

[1] See also xii, 1. Cf. Aquinas, *Sum. Theol.*, I, 108, 1 concl.: "Omnes angeli et rationales creaturae unius sunt hierarchiae."

Rome to her destruction he is referring to this larger strategy. Neither is this view peculiar to St. Augustine. Thus we find in St. Paul not only the conception of a society of the holy, but that of a kingdom of evil, or, less abstractly, of evil wills, evil persons. Hence he says that our battle is not with flesh and blood but with principalities and powers.

Augustine's doctrine of the angels is, then, well founded in Scripture and raises a number of curious problems both for the interpretation and philosophy of history, and for metaphysics. How far we need go with him in the details of his interpretation of men's actions, where he makes appeal to an angelic agency in a concrete instance, is another matter. And when, for instance (xxi, 6), he holds that there can be a magical communication between men and devils, some may prefer to leave the question open.

The metaphysical problems are not systematically raised by St. Augustine and are best treated by St. Thomas. The student should run his eye down the theses listed under *angelus* in a good index to the *Summa Theologica*. If the intervention of angels in human affairs is to be rationally credible then we must be able to understand how causes in different orders can produce the same effect while leaving each cause its own proper efficacy. For instance, we must be able to understand how the success in business of a man, A, can both be due to his own efforts, and yet be achieved by an angel, B, in pursuit of the latter's concerns, without any diminution of A's causality. When St. Thomas holds that the angels govern all the operations of the physical universe[1] he wishes, not to deny that there is an autonomous realm of physical law, but to assert that every event which occurs occurs in a hierarchy of dimensions. For instance, if we split an atom something is happening in a moral as well as a physical dimension. If I saw through a plank the partition of the plank is brought about by the saw as a physical agent, and also by my

[1] *Sum. Theol.*, I, 110, 1.

intentions as an artisan. In fact, the physical event would not
have happened without the spiritual event, though this in no
way alters the laws of its physicality. But I see much more than
the saw of what is going on. The metaphysical problem of the
angels is whether a superior agent with a much wider vision than
mine can stand to my causality as mine stands to that of the saw.
In the last resort the metaphysical problems of Providence are
raised: whether God can be said to do all things, with an all-
encompassing vision, but with no diminution of the proper
powers of inferior agents, including the free causality of men. In
the mind of St. Augustine this is possible. For him, the explosion
of the Hiroshima bomb would have been not only a physical
event but an event in the dimensions of human, angelic and
divine politics. We can achieve an intelligible explanation at all
these levels though in the last event only God knows why it happened, and the highest glimpse we can get at the reasons is
through His mind as revealed to us. Augustine is not trying to
obliterate the ordinary procedures of the empirical historian,
but to remind us that human history takes place in a wider
matrix, and that we can write it at a higher level if we look at it
from the point of view to which God raises us by grace. Events
form one constellation from a purely human point of view and
another from the point of view of grace. The *City of God* is an
attempt to see the meaning of human affairs from the latter
point of view.

I have dwelt on these points at a length which may seem dis-
proportionate, because it gives us a glimpse of the largeness of
Augustine's universe, because we must see the role of the angels
from Augustine's point of view, and because it lays some founda-
tions for what must subsequently be said. We can return now to
the argument of Book XI.

We can best regard the ensuing chapters of Book XI as a rich ^{XI, 10 ff.}
collection of thematic material much of which will be used later
on. Augustine's mind leaps from the doctrine of the Trinity to

the bliss and misery of the angels, and from this to the metaphysical structure of the universe, in a manner at first sight incoherent and confusing. Let us try to gather the threads.

He has said that the sole Cause of the universe is God. Since an effect is bound to reflect the nature of its cause, the more we can know about the cause the more we shall know about the structure of the effects, and this we desire to know because we are in quest of the structure of the *Civitas Dei*. Now we know from revelation that the true God is a Trinity, a unity of three Persons in the simplicity of one substance. God is Himself, knows Himself, and loves Himself. Christ is the Logos or Word of God, the Wisdom of God, begotten of the being of God Himself, who is con-substantial with His own Logos. The third Person is the Holy Spirit, who is the love by which the Father and the Son are united.[1]

The world is created by the triune God, and must itself bear the stamp of its Creator. Further, happiness consists in turning to God. At its highest it is a contemplation or seeing of God, and the nature of this contemplation will depend on the nature of its object. Since the *Civitas Dei* is the society of those who turn to God we must explain how the Holy Trinity is reflected in it. The happiness of the angels arises from their being in the presence of God. "These holy angels learn not of God by sounds, but by being present with that unchangeable truth, His only-begotten Word, Himself, and His Holy Spirit, that undivided Trinity." Further, they see whatever is created in its cause, and so "referring all those works to the Creator's praise, it shines like morning in the minds of these contemplators". (ch. 29.) For men, too, Augustine holds, the highest happiness is illumination by the Truth or Word of God, a seeing of things in Christ.

Now men and angels can defect from their own happiness. More of this anon. Yet in so doing they defect from their own

---

[1] It is not within the compass of the commentator to write a treatise on the Trinity at this point. The uninstructed can break the ice with C. S. Lewis's *Beyond Personality* and proceed to F. J. Sheed's *Theology and Sanity*.

natures, whose very metaphysical structure is trinitarian. This is true not only of intelligences but right down the scale of being to material things. The world owes its origin to God's goodness and "if this goodness be now the Holy Spirit, then is all the whole Trinity intimated to us in every creature." (xi, 24.)

This structure is discernible in man even if we take him without the perfections bestowed by grace. "We have in ourselves an image of that Holy Trinity for we both [1] have a being [2], know it, and [3] love both our being and our knowledge." (xi, 26.) "I know that I am myself, that this I know and love ... 'What if you err?' If I err, I am. For he that has no being cannot err, and therefore my error proves my being." Augustine is certain, against any academic scepticism, that he and every other man is, knows, and loves his being and his knowing.

Even animals, plants and stones show this threefold mark implanted in them by the divine love. "What of brute beasts ... do they not show their love of being, by avoiding death in all ways possible? The trees and plants that have no sense of death nor means to avoid it, do they not put forth one sprig into the air, and another deeper into the earth, whereby to attract nutriment and preserve their being? Nay, the very bodies that have neither sense nor vegetation by their very motion ... move to the conservation of their essence and nature." (xi, 27.) Even the action and causality of inanimate matter, then, is a reception and expression of the creative work of the Trinity, and to understand it at the highest level we must see it as such. Indeed, all the sciences can through this way be reduced to theology.[1]

Even this pencil in my hand, then, has a trinitarian structure. It is, and echoes eternity by persisting.[2] It participates in wisdom, in *logos* or discourse, because it has a structure which can be known or spoken about. It "professes a desire to be known since it cannot know itself", and this vicarious self-knowledge by an

[1] This doctrine of the illumination of all things in Christ, and of the reduction of all the sciences to theology, is a perennial characteristic of Augustinianism.
[2] "Suique similis in quantum potest esse conetur." (*De Musica*, vi, ch. xvii, §56.)

intelligence constitutes science, which is therefore only possible through the Word of God. Thirdly, its love of itself is expressed by those very physical characteristics by which it asserts and preserves itself as itself. "The motions of weights are like their bodies' loves, go they upward or downwards: for weight is to the body as love is to the soul." (xi, 28.)[1] The very manifestations of gravity are a kind of love affair, and even mechanics is founded in romance.

The image of God, then, is omnipresent, and the divine love is the substance of every being. Beholding it everywhere we "recall our thoughts home", where "our being shall have no end, our knowledge no error, our love no offence". Every creature is thus a beacon to the holy city which (1) *is*, by God's creation, (2) has wisdom by God's enlightenment and (3) is happy by inhering in God by love (xi, 24).

It will be observed that Augustine does not condemn all self-love. On the contrary. He had to do justice to the Scriptural text which tells us to love others as we love ourselves, where love of self appears to be the norm of other-love. Since we are beings we are the proper objects of love and of our own love. Now what makes us lovable is that the image of the Trinity is stamped upon us, so that what we legitimately love is the image of God in ourselves, or ourselves in our proper subordination to God. As self-conscious, we have an immediate apprehension of that resemblance in ourselves, and this makes it possible for us to see and love that resemblance in others. Hence legitimate self-love enables us to love others in God.

There is, however, a false self-love which is an inordinate love of ourselves, and which is the source of concupiscence. We can by a misuse of our wills love ourselves as though we were our own good, referring all other men and goods, and even God, to ourselves as centre. They become things to be used for our own

---

[1] Cf. *De Musica*, vi, ch. §29: "Delectatio quippe quasi pondus est animae. Delectatio ergo ordinat animam ... ubi autem cor, ibi beatitudo aut miseria."

aggrandisement. This is the self-love of pride which makes an original of an image, and sees the world and God as a projection of itself, viewing everything in relation to its own interests.

There is then an *amor sui* which is an *amor Dei*, and relates a man to the world seen as a fellowship; and an *amor sui* which, enclosing a man within himself, renders him incapable of any right relations.

Augustine says that the *civitas terrena* was established by the defection of some of the angels. This brings him up against the question of the origin of evil, which is considered in Book XII. The discussion involves the notions of (a) a hierarchy of beings or natures and (b) a hierarchy of values, and some remarks on these orders will be valuable. We can use xi, 16 as the peg on which to hang them.

Augustine accepts the notion of a universe which is graded XI, 16 according to ontological superiority and inferiority. Some things are better *by nature* than others. By nature angels are better than men, men than beasts, beasts than plants, plants than inanimate matter. This is a hierarchy created by God, and it would be simply untrue to say, for instance, that in the order of nature a beast was better than a man. A man would offend against truth were he to say that he was worse than a dog, neither would it be licit for him to say that he would rather be a dog than a man.

On the other hand we have to distinguish the order of nature from the order of values. By nature all angels are better than all men. By nature the worst devil is better than the best man. By another standard, however, the *lex iustitiae* as compared with the *ordo naturae*, a good man stands higher than a bad angel. We are right in preferring a good man to a bad angel.

In our ordinary affairs we frequently display such preferences. "Who had not rather have his pantry full of meat than mice, or possess pence than fleas?" Whether these ordinary preferences are licit Chapter 16 leaves us in some doubt. If we value things according to nature, says Augustine, we are "valuing them by the light of the mind"; while if we take them relatively to human needs we are valuing them "by the pleasure or use of the sense".

Prima facie at any rate this statement will not bear consideration—if, that is, we are to assume that the light of the mind is to be preferred to the pleasure of the senses. The Bishop of Hippo would doubtless have preferred a stewed rabbit to a live one on his dinner plate; and if we have Franciscan doubts about that, at any rate it seems clear that if a beggar asks us for pence we should not give him a handful of fleas on the grounds that fleas were by nature more valuable. Every time we boil a carrot or kill a fowl we are preferring the order of use to the order of nature. Further, we consider this preference *reasonable*. It is true, however, that this order of use is based on the order of nature. My right to kill a carrot rests on my being better by nature. It is wrong for me to murder, no matter how bad my victim, because I am not better by nature.

If that is what Augustine really means in this chapter then it makes sense. At any rate certain important distinctions emerge. We must distinguish the order of values from the order of nature, and the order of use from the ontological hierarchy. Now the order of use involves the will in a manner in which the order of nature does not. If I prefer pence to fleas the choice is relative to my purposes, and my purposes may be good or bad. My preference for pence may under some circumstances be wrong, but it cannot be wrong simply because, objectively, fleas are better than pence. *What makes the purpose right or wrong?* Augustine holds that vice arises from undue preferences. But what makes them undue? In an indirect, if not in the direct, way we must come back to the order of nature. I may licitly prefer a cabbage's life to a rabbit's. As a farmer, for instance, I may have to kill the rabbits in my cabbage patch. But would I have a right to kill a man simply because he stole some cabbages? His action is morally worse than the rabbit's, yet it is ontologically superior, being a manifestation of will and intelligence. It may be more damaging, but I have to respect the nature of the agent. If, *per impossible*, I could kill Satan I should have no right to do so. Even God, who has the power, does not do so.

It would appear then that the bounds are set to our purposes by the nature of certain ontological structures. Usableness for our purposes must be confined to the things of sense.[1] But when it comes to the bearers of purposes, namely, free intelligent beings, we are subject to the criterion of position in the scale of nature. We may not regard ourselves or other men, or angels, or God, as mere utilities for our own wills. This is the real case against a magical utilization of a higher order of beings. To commit sin or vice, then, is to go against the order of nature, and consequently against the will of God who established it. It is to misuse the order of things, radically to prefer the inferior to the superior, to make a mistake about what manner of beings we are. We *prefer* ourselves in a realm where preference has been taken from us by the nature of things, and where preference must give way to praise. I may licitly prefer pence to fleas, or fleas to pence, but I cannot licitly prefer *to be* God or an angel or even another man. I may licitly prefer to be good rather than evil, but that is only because in preferring to be good I am submitting to the given purpose of my nature. It is better for a given man to be that man and not an angel, though an angel is by nature higher than a man. Further, it would be wrong to try to behave like an angel, at any rate with respect to an angel's *differentia*. But it is better to be a good man than a bad angel, goodness being a matter of choice and nature not. But in both cases it is better because God's ordinances are the rule of right and wrong, and in the latter case because those ordinances have been explicitly accepted. To be good is to achieve a congruity between what we think and will, and the ontological fact that our being is a received being,[2] in a certain position in the scale

---

[1] This issue appears prominently in Book XIX.
[2] "Ut sibi amica natura sit." (xix, 13.)

of God's creation. In the last resort value is dictated by being.

Let us try to sum this up succinctly.

(a) There is an order of nature or of creation which we can represent as follows:

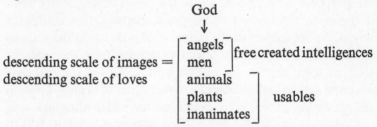

(b) There is an objective order of values which corresponds to the order of being or nature. Men are in themselves more valuable than animals, plants than stones.

(c) There is a subjective order of valuations. Free created intelligences are under an obligation to recognize the order of nature, and to prefer beings in accordance with their objective order. They have the power, not to alter the order of nature, but to evaluate or not to evaluate things according to their objective order.

(d) There is an order of use. Things lacking freedom are usable. Thus man has a right to use things below him in the order of nature. He is not obliged to follow the order of nature in his preferences. He may prefer pence to fleas. Nevertheless his preferences must ultimately be with a view to the order of nature. Things are rightly used only for God.

(e) There is a true *amor sui*, which is at the same time an *amor proximi* and an *amor Dei*. It is a seeing of oneself and of all things according to the objective order of creation, that is, as a scale of images dependent on an Original. It proceeds from a will which gives its just due to the order willed by God.

(f) There is a false *amor sui*, or *amor concupiscentiae*. A free intelligence is able to posit itself as the original, and to see everyone and everything else, including God, as a projection of, or means to, or image of, itself. It is egocentric love.

The effect of egocentric love is to degrade all reality to the category of the usable, with oneself as the end. Thus man is preferred to God, the angels are harnessed by magical practices, other men are exploited, and the things which are properly usable are not used for God but for the lusts of the self-enclosed ego.

III

BOOK XII: ANGELS, MEN AND SIN

IN Book XI Augustine has told us about the origin of the heavenly city by a divine creative act. He has told us that the angels are its first inhabitants, and he has laid down many of his fundamental principles. The *De Civitate Dei*, however, is a tale of two cities, a heavenly and an earthly, a good and an evil. We have now to deal with the rise of the latter. It comes into being through a spiritual fall of angels and of men. Book XII deals mainly with the former and Book XIII with the latter.

What now confronts us is the question of the origin of evil, a question which had always deeply engaged St. Augustine. He was a man both of fine conscience and of strong passions who knew what it was both to love deeply and to love wrongly. He knew the disruptive force of evil both in personal and political life, and it became a matter of life and death for him to deal with it both in life and in thought. In Book XII he attacks the question of how evil came to infect the angelic beings.

Certain of the guiding principles have already been laid down. We have to do with a universe created *ex nihilo* by a good and omnipotent God, and in which there is a scale of beings which is also a scale of worth. Intelligent beings can grasp their own worth and actively place themselves where they belong. They can place a value on themselves and on other beings, and exercise by will a preference according to their valuations.

In this book, as frequently in the *De Civitate Dei*, Augustine insists that every being or nature is a praise of God (cf. xii, v).

It is as it were an echo of the love by which God loves Himself. Augustine's insistence upon this can be fully understood only in the light of his Manichean past.[1] The Manichees were dualists who acknowledged a Kingdom of Light and a Kingdom of Darkness. Their founder, Mani, was born in A.D. 216 in Babylonia, and believed that he had received a revelation that he was the Holy Ghost. He endeavoured to spread a gnostic,[2] spiritual religion, influenced by the Persian conception of two co-eternal principles of light and darkness in strife with each other. The kingdom of evil is composed of natures evil in themselves, and the realm of matter is radically evil. In man the strife manifests itself as the battle between flesh and spirit. Moral evil arises in us from the taint of the body.

Augustine's conversion struggles led him to the discovery of full human responsibility. One could not off-load the responsibility for one's sins on something extraneous to the will, namely, the body. What confronts us in ourselves is one nature divided against itself. "When I was deliberating about serving the Lord my God, as I had long meant to do, it was I who willed to do it, I who was unwilling. It was I. I did not wholly will, I was not wholly unwilling." (*Conf.*, viii, 10.) "Lord, give me chastity," he cries out, "but not yet." *Unde hoc monstrum?* From wherever it may be, the escape from it shows itself in the ability of the will to will the good whole-heartedly.

The Christian doctrine of creation did away with the Manichean dualism of nature. Since the *sole* cause of every being is God there can be nothing in any being which is not good. "I know besides that wherein the vicious will is resident, therein is that done, which, if the will would not, should not be done ... It is not the thing to which we fall, but our fall that is evil: that is, we fall to no evil natures, but against nature's order, from the

[1] For an account of the Manichees see J. J. O'Meara, *The Young Augustine*, London, Longmans, 1954, ch. iv.

[2] Gnosticism is the belief that salvation is through a special and esoteric knowledge.

highest to the lower. Herein is evil. Covetousness is no vice in the gold, but in him that perversely leaves justice to love gold ... Nor is lust the fault of sweet beauteous bodies, but the soul's that runs perversely to bodily delights." (xii, 8.)

The fundamental innocence of subhuman nature is thus established. It speaks of nothing but its Creator's goodness. There is a comparison possible between Augustine's praise of created nature in the *Confessions* and the hymn to the sun of St. Francis written at the time of the Manichean revival among the Albigenses. Augustine is of course aware that subhuman nature is a process where there is generation and corruption, and where some beings live at the expense of others, but he asks us not to see in nature only a realm of universal cannibalism with which man is desperately at war (xii, 4). In nature there is decay and corruption. But we must consider that "earthly things are not comparable to heavenly: yet might not the world be without them, because the others are more glorious." That is, the existence even of inferior and imperfect beings, of a grand scale of creation from high to low, is a greater witness to God than a less profuse creation. The lowest being is still more than nothing, and therefore it is better that it should be than that it should not be. It could not be without the frailty which goes with the very nature of a lowly thing. To have such beings means to have them as they are. To wish to have them incorruptible and immutable is a contradiction. It is really to wish not to have them at all. We must stand back from our petty and utilitarian preoccupations and see the grandeur and munificence of the total scale. If God created corruptible things it was not because He was ungenerous or impotent but because there is *no* bound to His liberality. He is willing to give even the smallest and most ephemeral trifles. Generation-and-corruption has its own beauties. It carries with it the charm of renewal, of sunrise and sunset, the movement of the sea, the seasons, all exhibiting orders and rhythms inexhaustible to the mind. "It is not the consideration of nature in respect of our profit, but as it is in itself, that glorifies the Creator."

We have in Augustine a genuine theistic vision of nature very different from the pantheistic world of Spinoza. Whereas Spinoza sees in our experience of beauty nothing more than a subjective affection of the imagination born of our preoccupation with ourselves, Augustine recognizes that while we remain locked in our own subjectivity we are much more likely to see ugliness and hurt than beauty; that, in more modern language, beauty is an objective value, and that we must stand back from the picture if we wish to discern its intrinsic rhythms and composition. Augustine does not oppose the order of beauty and the order of reason in the manner of Spinoza in the appendix to *Ethica* I. On the contrary, he brings them together. He recognizes the limitations of the human standpoint, and in the *De Musica* he uses the following examples. If one were placed like a statue in a corner of a large house, one would not be in a position to enjoy the architectural beauties of the whole edifice. Again, the soldier confined to his particular function cannot appreciate the order of the whole army. Or yet again, if in a poem the syllables had life and feeling for the time of their enunciation, they could not enjoy the continuity of the whole poem. The beauty and harmony of the universe is for Augustine precisely *not* something subjective. But as subjects we have an objective ontological status which prevents our seeing the whole edifice. The limitation of our view is thus objectively determined. It depends on our placing. And from the fact of our placing and from the fragments of harmony which we can discern from thence, we can argue to the existence of a creative beauty who has made all things in number, order, and measure.

The scale of being is a hierarchical scale of beings each of which is one and is good. It is one because it is in the image of the one God. Furthermore, the totality of the universe is one and for the same reason. It could, however, not be one were its XII, 2 parts not interconnected. Like the Platonic universe, it is a harmony. God utters it in time like a piece of verse. The principle of its interconnection, of its order, is hierarchy. You cannot take degree away from it. Natures stand to each other in degrees of subordination and superordination. "For since God is the highest essence, that is, wholly is, and therefore is immutable, He granted it to His creatures, which He made out of nothing, to be; but not wholly to be, like Himself. To some He gave more being [*esse*], to others less, ordering the natures of beings in degrees." What we have is a universe in which some beings are nobler than others because their participation in the divine likeness is more explicit. We have essences diversely distanced from their source. Let us put it that God loves some beings better than others. A man is more lovable than a stone because God loves men better than stones and has created in and by that love. The scale of ontological worth is a scale of love. What we mean by saying that one thing is better than another is that it is more worthy of love. What holds the world together and gives it a unity is a system of attractions which derive from the attractiveness of God. "Weight is to a body, what love is to the soul." God, *qui summe est*, demands the highest love simply by virtue of being God. To love God and to be subordinate or obedient to Him are the same act viewed in two ways. And so down the whole scale of natures: what is lower owes an obedience to what is higher. Insubordination strikes at the roots of the cosmos itself. We may notice, by the way, how firmly Shakespeare has grasped this conception, and how often in his plays the unlawful outrage upon due authority is attended by storms and portents in nature.

Men and angels are higher than the subhuman universe because their obedience is not of necessity but of will. Natural necessity is the due expression of the loves of stones. Intelligent beings must apprehend their purposes in truth and give their love in freedom. It is because they are more like God, higher in the scale of being, that they are responsible for making their acts correspond with their position.

The highest good of intelligent beings is to adhere freely to XII, 1 God in love, and to love in other creatures the intentions of God in them. The good angels were those who "persisted in God, their common good". The evil angels were those who "delighting more in their own power, as though it were from themselves, fell from that common all-blessing good to dote upon their own and ... became proud, deceitful and envious." The source of the angelic evil, then, is a will freely misdirected, a rebellion against due authority.

For Augustine all vice, sin or evil is an outrage upon natures, or, what comes to the same thing, the disorganization of a hierarchy. All vice is against nature. A sinful being is a divided being, a being whose will is split by itself and against itself. It must be noted, however, that no nature can be contrary to God, but only a will. It is precisely because the will does not square with the nature that the person is disintegrated. "The Scripture calls them God's enemies, because they oppose His sovereignty not by nature but will, having no power to hurt Him but themselves." (xii, 3.) The devils remain superior to man by nature. We must contemn their wills but may not contemn their natures, which continue to praise God by virtue of what they are. In this sense the love of God persists even in hell.

Further, though there can be good without evil there cannot be evil without good. "Vice cannot be in the highest good, nor can it be but in some good." There must be something for it to hurt or damage. A non-entity cannot be evil. Vice is as it were parasitic upon good. It exists as a perversion. Devils are perverts. Vice cannot destroy nature except by destroying itself.

Readers who come to Augustine from Plato will notice the great area of resemblance in spite of the difference of atmosphere. For both thinkers the cosmos is hierarchically ordered. In Plato the ultimate principle of its unity and order is the good with which the soul can be united by an ascent through love and knowledge. For both the end of vice is a tyranny which perverts the hierarchy, and for both vice displays itself in an insubordination of goods, a preference for the worse over the better. For both the evil is parasitic upon the good, and for both the inversion of the hierarchy means social and personal disintegration. In spite of the lack of explicit reference it is impossible to doubt that Augustine's classical background plays a considerable part in the construction of the *De Civitate Dei*. Socrates' argument against Thrasymachus—that wrong-doing is an offence against measure, and that a nature exerts its proper virtue and power only under law—has been thoroughly incorporated into the book. Augustine prefers to quote the Psalmist where he says: "Thou madest all things in number, weight and measure" (xi, 30), but he moulds the words of revelation with Greek instruments.

Like Plato, then, Augustine holds that there is no being which is not being-in-order. It is a conception which we find throughout his works. There are some striking expressions of it in the *De Musica*, where its Pythagorean and Platonic affiliations are clear. He argues there that the universe itself is a harmony of "numbers" reflecting the divine One. "Where there is equality and similitude, there is numbered order [*numerositas*]. For there is nothing more equal or like than a one to a one." (vi, ch. xiii, §38.) Harmony is made or found in nature because it is present in the soul, and the soul is enlightened by God who is the one Creator of all things. Each thing, being like God, is also a one, but so is the totality of creation, each thing being placed, like a syllable in a verse, by the nature of the whole as a single structure made by the divine Word. Commenting on the verse *Deus, creator omnium* in the same work (vi, ch. xvii, §57), Augustine paints a picture of the rhythms both of art and of nature, and asks: "Whence, I ask you, do these things come unless from that supreme and eternal Principle of numbers and similitude, and equality and order? If you take away these properties from the world there will be nothing." We find the same argument in the *De Libero Arbitrio*.[1] "Look at the sky and the earth and the sea, and whatever shines brightly above or creeps below or flies or swims. They have forms because they have numbers. Take these away, and nothing will be left. What is their source but the source of number? For, so far as they have being, they have numbered being."

In the two works just mentioned Augustine is speaking as a philosopher rather than a theologian. He offers us a rational proof of God's existence based on our experience of art, freedom and nature. In the *De Civitate Dei*, however, it is the theologian who is uppermost, and who proceeds from revelation to nature. This is the strikingly un-Platonic element in his procedure, though there is perhaps more of it in Plato than we are sometimes led to believe. In any event Augustine is more opposed to neo-Platonism as a theology than to Platonism as a philosophy and his animus is frequently an *odium theologiae*.

Let us get back, however, to angelic sin. Following Scripture, Augustine holds that before man sinned the angels had already sinned. Further, those who sinned sinned because their wills were evil, not their natures. What they did was to prefer some other good than God as their highest good. In fact, the good which they preferred was the excellence of their own natures. "They delighted more in their own power".[2] This is the sin of pride which is the root of the diabolic malice. Pride, then, is the primordial sin.

This, then, is what the angelic sin consists in. We have now to raise the question how it could come about. Clearly, if God is both good and omnipotent it is reasonable to ask how He could have created a universe which He must have foreknown would be blemished by sin.

[1] ii, xvi, 42.
[2] "Quo vitio Deum imitari, quam Deo servire anima maluit." (*De Musica*, vi, xiii, §40.)

Deeply considered this reduces to the question: Why did God create at all? For as soon as there was a creation the possibility of sin was there. It was there because every creature has as it were an admixture of nothingness in its composition. It participates not only in being but in non-being. The possibility of a relapse is given with its very nature. Why did God create such beings? The answer has in fact already been given. We must ascribe this creation not to any impotence or maleficence in the divine action, but to the unbounded generosity of God who, willing the *fullness* of being, wills it down to its most trifling manifestation. His love of being is such that He utters it on the fullest scale. An imperfect being is better than a non-entity, and since God wills the best He wills the better. That there are beings capable of corruption and damnation witnesses therefore to the omnipotent goodness of God.

How is it, then, that it is the best creatures, the free intelligences, who corrupt the world with evil? For corruption proceeds not from matter upwards but from Lucifer downwards. The astonishing answer is: Because God made them good. They sin because they are the most like God, because God loves them best. What do we mean by this? The world is a hierarchy in which God is imaged in ascending degrees. The higher we go the clearer is the image of God. Now God is a free Creator who creates gratuitously. The beings most like Him will be those who in their degree have a derived power of free creativity. That is, those who are most obviously dependent on God, will have the highest degree of proper causality, and in that sense, of independence. The potentiality of a fall will be greatest where it is least justified because there the power and goodness of God is most manifest.

Further, the proper object of the will is the good, and the will is most firmly held by what is best. Now the angelic nature is the most excellent of created natures, and therefore the most attractive to the angelic will. Because it is the most like God it is the

most easily substituted for God. Pride consists in the substitution of the image for the original, but the substitution is
possible only because of the generosity with which God has
bestowed essence on the image. With respect, then, both to
the power of the will and to its object, the possibility of sin
bears witness to the power and goodness of God, and not to
any defect in Him. The very defects of creatures are a praise
of God.

But we are still faced with the question why a possibility
rooted in the structure of created being should have been
realized, why a disvalue should have been subjectively appro-
priated. In a sense, the question is quite unanswerable, because
freedom remains a mystery. Every free act is a new creation
analogous to God's act of creation, and participates in the
mystery of the superabundance of the divine being. In fact, all
causality is in the last resort mysterious. *Natura id agit interiore
motu, nobisque occultissimo.* Man puts in operation what God
has given, rather as we may drive a car without knowing how
it works.

Yet we must point out that the question may be illegitimately
formulated. We ask: What is the cause of the evil will? But so
to pose it is immediately to assume what Augustine has been at
great pains to deny—that evil has a nature—because only an
entity can have a cause. Hence he says: "Let none therefore seek
the efficient cause of an evil will; for it is not efficient but defi-
cient, nor is there any effect but defect, namely falling from that
highest essence unto a lower ... The causes whereof, if one endeavour to seek, it is as if he should seek to see the darkness." If
evil then is not a nature, it must be nothing. "Because his will
was made of nothing, he shall find that his evil arose not from
his nature but from nothing." (xii, 7, §6.) Evil is present in a
nature not as something, but as a lack of something which that
nature should have. One might say that the presence of evil in
a nature is really an absence, so that evil is not a nature but a

privation of being. Willing evilly is a lapse, a failure to act, rather than an act, since action proceeds from being, and to be is to be in order. Evil acts therefore are known by not knowing, and known are still unknown (xii, 7), because only beings are knowable, and not privations.

When Augustine says, then, that evil is a privation or that evil is nothing he must be very strictly understood. It is not a way of minimizing it or reducing it to appearance, but of emphasizing its terrible element of sheer destructiveness. No one is further than Augustine from denying what we should call the reality of evil, but it remains true that its striking force is rooted in the good. If a man tortures me he is committing, and I am suffering, an evil. But the man can torture me effectively only insofar as he is good and uses means which in themselves are good. Steel is good, fire is good, and so is the intelligence and ingenuity with which they are applied to me. Ontologically considered, and as far as his act is an act, it is good. His action is evil because of something lacking in the man and in the act, namely, good will. Likewise the evil produced in me by torture is a deprivation of bodily integrity. It renders me less than I should be. I suffer as good, that is, as having consciousness, a sensitive body, and so on. It is the absence of what is no longer in me that is evil. To do evil is always a failure to do something or to be something.

v, 9, 10   The defence of freedom against those who say that created freedom is incompatible with God's foreknowledge, and against those who maintain that our actions are dictated by necessity, is not undertaken in Book XII. It has already been dealt with in v, 9 and 10. In Chapter 9 Augustine joins issue with Cicero for arguing that "if all events were known before they came to pass, they should come to pass according to that foreknowledge. And if they come so to pass, then God knows the certain order of things beforehand ... then are all events disposed by fate." Nothing is left in the power of our wills, to the destruction of all responsibility, law, reward, praise and blame. To confirm man in his dignity as free we must therefore deny the divine foreknowledge. Augustine, on the contrary, holds that God both foreknew that angels and men would fall, and that He did not cause them to fall. "God doth both know all things ere they come to pass, and we do all things willingly, which we do not feel ourselves and know ourselves directly enforced to." He argues that our wills are causes whose operation is foreknown by God, but He knows them precisely as the causes of their actions. He knows them in their freedom. Further, in an argument of singular relevance at the present day, he warns us not to transfer considerations of causality drawn from subhuman nature to the realm of freedom, since subhuman nature is rather in our power than we in its. "How can that set order of causes in God's foreknowledge deprive our wills of power, seeing our wills bear such a sway amongst the very causes themselves?" God established our wills as causes of a higher kind, so that our wills are free not in spite of God's foreknowledge but rather because of it.

He goes on to point out that we cannot will against our wills. We *must* be free. But even this cannot be given a necessitarian interpretation. We use such language of God Himself. Thus we say that He *must* have foreknowledge, that He cannot die, and that He cannot err. But to be able to do these things He would have to be less than God, that is, not be omnipotent. "He cannot do some things because He can do all things." *Mutatis mutandis*, this applies to us. That we must will freely witnesses to our power as causes, and not to any impotence. We have the power which God foreknew we should have, and without that dependence we could exercise no independence. God foreknows our sins but we do not sin because God foreknows it, but because we have the freedom to refuse the subordination in which is spiritual freedom.

These questions are more fully dealt with in the *De Libero*

Arbitrio, which is easily accessible in translation,[1] and which pursues philosophic interests which came later to seem to Augustine of less importance.

XII, 10 ff. Having dealt with the angelic creation, freedom and fall, Augustine turns his attention to the human situation. We shall be content to notice very briefly what the drift of the argument is.

Before dealing with the creation of man Augustine has to deal with the creation of the world in which he lives. He rebuts the theory that the world has existed *ab aeterno*, and that it will endure through various cycles to eternity. He maintains on the contrary that man was made less than six thousand years ago and that God will put a definite term to history. We must notice specially his vehement rejection of Greek cyclical theories of the course of the universe, and the notions of eternal return and repetition. While we shall not develop the subject here,[2] this rejection is of great importance for Augustine's theology of history, and marks the predominance of Hebrew over Greek notions in his mind. The Jews had a linear conception of history which goes together with their sense of the uniqueness of historical events. We may grasp this better if we glance briefly at some other viewpoints. In writing the history of the Peloponnesian War Thucydides was endeavouring to extract certain general truths or essences from the events which he described. How will an imperialist democracy react under pressures of a certain kind, what is the nature of the class war, what will be the fate of moderates in a revolution? Again in *Republic* VIII and IX Plato is endeavouring to construct a diagram which will cover all cases of political decline. If we jump the centuries and look at the refutation of human free-will in Hume's *Treatise*, we shall find that Hume regards history as a vast quarry or laboratory which exhibits the unchanging mechanism of human reactions. And to come down to our own days, the central weak-

---

[1] *The Problem of Free Choice*, Ancient Christian Writers, London, Longmans, 1955.

[2] See Christopher Dawson, *Progress and Religion*, London, 1929.

ness of Toynbee's *Study of History* is his presentation of history
not as unique factuality but as a play of Platonic essences. He is
looking for "philosophic equivalents" in history, often failing
dismally to see the differentia of two historical situations, or of
two historical persons. For instance, having achieved the general-
ization "die-hard reactions", he assimilates the Vatican decrees
against modernism to the "militantly archaistic movements of
Wahhabism, Idrisism, Sanusism, and Mahdism". When a concrete historical complex becomes an -ism its functional character
in concrete history is lost. Again the specific character of Christianity is buried in the conception "universal religions". Christ
and Apollo become confused and the real vanishes in the ideal.

The Jew, on the other hand, related the occurrences of history
to the will of a Person, and attributed to them the uniqueness
which belongs to free acts. History is the progressive revelation
of a divine intention. Each event is a move in a drama which de-
ploys further the strategy of salvation. The Chosen People is
unique and its history unlike any other history. In the Christian
revelation Christ becomes the keystone of the drama. He is not
another saviour-god, but the absolute pivot of human affairs,
born in Bethlehem when Cyrinus was governor of Syria.

We have to remember that for Augustine Christ and salvation
were central realities, and that it is in the Incarnation that we
must look for the clue to history. The Incarnation gives time a
reality which it could not have for a Greek. If Christ was born
at a certain place at a certain time, time cannot be an illusion
or the realm of meaningless contingency. Cyrinus is assumed
into a realm of eternal importance. There is an ultimate meaning
to be discerned in human affairs, a meaning to be worked out in
time, a meaning which vanishes entirely if history is to repeat
itself in endless cycles for ever. There can be only one Christ and
therefore only one Cyrinus, and this extends to the very pencil
I am holding. The Incarnation governs Augustine's sense of time
and personality, and his great meditation on time in the

Confessions cannot be excised from the book without seriously weakening its weight as a discovery of personality and of will.

The key to these chapters may with some justification be said to be found towards the end of xii, 13. "Plato the Athenian philosopher taught in the academy that in a certain unbounded space, yet definite, Plato himself, his scholars, the city and school, should after infinite ages meet all in that place again and be as they were when he taught this. God forbid, I say, that we should believe this. 'For Christ once died for our sins, and rising again, dies no more'." "The wicked walk in a circuit", but in the Christian life the revolutions have no place. "The saints' eternal life overthrows them utterly." In one of his great paradoxes Augustine says of God *novit quiescens agere et agens quiescere* (xii, 17). God is the endless peace who is endless activity drawing mankind with a sure design to a final consummation in His eternity where the meaning and salvation of history will be achieved for ever.

The reader should, therefore, not be put off or misled by Augustine's biblical literalism about the date of man's creation. The question at issue is very much larger. It is the question whether man may be said to have a history which is ultimately meaningful. If he has, then it must have an end, and if it has an end it must have had beginning. Just how we are to interpret "beginning" is a further matter, but Augustine's argument is moving on another level than that of the condition of the science contemporary to him or to us.

IV

BOOK XIII: THE FALL OF MAN AND
ITS CONSEQUENCES

HAVING dealt with the question of the origin of the world and of man Augustine goes on to talk about the fall of man. If the fall of the angels establishes the *civitas terrena* in the heavens, then the fall of man establishes it on earth. Augustine holds that like the angels man was created in a state of pristine goodness or grace which he too forfeited by a misuse of his will. But he does not immediately proceed to discuss this event but to describe one of its consequences, the consequence of mortality.

The angels were created immortal, and even sin could not take that immortality from them. Man has by nature an immortal *soul*, but *man*, who is body as well as soul, is capable of death. What we ordinarily call death is the dissolution of the body, but Augustine holds, following Scripture, that the soul can also die a kind of death. Man is capable therefore of a double death, the first of which, since the Fall, is the lot of every man, and the second the lot only of the wicked. The death of the body is when the soul leaves it, the death of the soul when God leaves it. The soul may be dead before the body dies, and such is the condition of soul of the wicked. The death of the soul is absolutely an evil; the death of the body, while relatively an evil, can be a good to the good if their wills are rightly disposed to it. Even baptismal regeneration does not remove from us the evil of bodily death. It remains an evil. But the just man can use even what is evil well, while the unjust will use even a good evilly. A martyr, for instance, uses death well; an evil man uses a good, like intelligence for instance, to his damnation.

In addition to this double death, Augustine recognizes a "second death" wherein the soul, reunited to the body in the general resurrection, shall together with it endure an eternity of pain. We thus have

1 { 1. Death of the body.
    2. Death of the soul, which may occur in this life by our desertion of God.

2 { 3. The second death, which is the final and last perdition. (See esp. xiii, 12.)

Further, this life is a realm of death. "As soon as ever man enters this mortal body, he begins a perpetual journey unto death. For that this changeable life enjoins him to, if I may call the course unto death a life ... Each part of time that we pass, cuts off so much from our life, and the remainder still decreases". (xiii, 10.) Man is always dying. His life is a *Sein zum Tode*. Again we must turn to the *Confessions*, Book IV, if we want to study the birth of Augustine's sense of death. It is the book in which he describes his experience of the death of a friend, an experience which must have done much to deepen his sense of the paradoxical character of our world. "In whatever I looked at," he says, "I saw death." *Factus eram ipse mihi magna questio*: I myself became to myself a great puzzle. Man is confronted with the agonizing puzzle of his own perpetual dying, which colours whatever he does and looks at, and which poses in the most dramatic way the problems of sin and evil. His sense of paradox, his sense of time and his sense of the mystery of the human personality come together indissolubly in XIII, 11, where he is discussing the problem whether one may be living and dead both together. "Dying before death come, he is not, for then he is living; dying when death is come, he is not, for then he is dead. The one is after death, and the other is before it. When is he in death, then? For he is in death when dying, to equate three things, *living*, *dying*, and *dead*, with three times *before death*, *in death*, and *after*. Therefore when he is in death, that is, neither living, or before death, nor dead, or after death, is hard to be defined." So great become the enigmas with which he burns that he calls out: "I would to God we had lived well in Paradise that death might have been nothing indeed. But now, there is not only such a thing, but it is so grievous unto us, as neither tongue can tell nor reason avoid."

We see then why the consideration of death precedes Augustine's account of man's fall. In his personal experience it was the phenomenon which brought home to him the misery of man's condition, and urged him to seek an explanation for his unhappy state. *O monstrum vitae et mortis profunditas!* Life is infected with the horrible mystery of death. It is human evil in the form that most needs accounting for.

Much in Book XIII anticipates what is said more fully later, but there are a few points in the ensuing chapters which can be briefly mentioned now. Augustine holds that even bodily death, which is generally regarded as a natural phenomenon, is really a result of the deprivation of nature by the Fall. "Wherefore all Christians holding the Catholic faith believe that the bodily death lies upon mankind by no law of nature, but as a due punishment for sin". (xiii, 15.) The body of the first man was corrupted by his spiritual corruption, the body, to his shame, becoming insubordinate to his soul. Augustine suggests that the mechanism for the transmission of original sin must be so explained. "We had not our particular forms yet, but there was the seed of our natural propagation which being corrupted by sin must needs produce man of that same nature, the slave to death, and the object of just condemnation ."(xiii, 14.)

Finally he holds, against the Platonists, that the possession of a body is a good. To a Platonist the separation of soul and body cannot be penal, being merely the removal of an impediment to spiritual vision. Man however desires the completion of his being and a felicity in which his body, too, shall share. Eternal life, made possible for us by Christ's suffering of our death in His body, is to include a restoration of the body.

V

BOOK XIV: THE EFFECTS OF MAN'S DISOBEDIENCE

WE are still concerned with the taking root of the *civitas terrena* XIV, 1 upon earth. The City of God came to earth with the creation of the first man, the earthly city with his fall. The doctrine of monogenism is necessary to Augustine's doctrine of the unity of history and of its providential character. He draws from it a doctrine not entirely unlike that of the Stoics, a doctrine still to be echoed in the *De Monarchia* of Dante, that mankind is by nature one. Further, their unity of origin must indicate to them the duty of a concord of heart. Original sin brings the shattering of this unity and this concord, yet even so the fundamental division of the human race is a simple one. Men differ in nationality, language, race and tradition but basically they are either good or bad, and this division cuts across all the other differences, and makes of fallen man not many communities but two, each of which has its own end and desire. That a man should speak a different language or have a skin of another colour is of quite minor importance. What matters is his interior disposition. "There are but two sorts of men that do properly make the two cities we speak of; the one is of men that live accordingly to the flesh, and the other of those that live according to the spirit, each wishing, when they have attained their desire, to enjoy their own particular peace."

Living according to the flesh and to the spirit are scriptural XIV, 2 terms which at first sight are disagreeable with Augustine's defence of the natural goodness of the body. He has therefore to indicate more precisely what is meant by the words of Scripture. He concludes that the Scriptures are employing metonymy, that is, signifying a whole by a part, as when we indicate a king by his crown, or speak of so many heads, or so many souls when we mean so many people. "Flesh," he concludes, means "man", and "living according to the flesh" means "living according to man". When St. Paul enumerates the works of the flesh he mentions not only sins which are closely connected with the body, like fornication, drunkenness and gluttony, but also idolatry, envy, contention, sedition and others which we commit with our minds rather than with our bodies. In fact, Augustine points out, a man may live a puritanical or ascetic life in the service of some heresy or idolatry "and in avoiding fleshly lusts commit most damnable works of the flesh".

XIV, 3, 4, 5   We must, then, avoid saying like the Manichees that the flesh causes viciousness of soul. It is true that we find the corruptible body a burden, but it is not the body's nature which is burdensome but its corruption, and this is the effect and not the cause of sin. The devil is fleshless, yet he sinned and sins. It was not flesh which was the cause of the devil's pride, but a spiritual will. The heart of the matter is that a man must not live according to a man, nor an angel to an angel, but both according to God. An angel living according to an angel would still be living "according to the flesh", insofar as he makes his own nature and not God his highest good. The essence of sin is a spiritual act by which the will turns itself from God.

It will be seen, then, that while Augustine is no enemy to asceticism, he has nothing good to say for an asceticism which is based simply upon hatred of our bodiliness. The end of asceticism must be the final restoration of the body, and his doctrine is a serious warning to those who confuse goodness with "spirituality". The spiritual vices are the most serious, the most elusive, the most capable of assuming the appearance of their opposites. In his inimitable way he sums up the matter by say-

ing: "The flesh is good, but to leave the Creator and live according to this created good is the mischief; whether a man chooses
to live according to the body or the soul or both ... For he that
makes the soul's nature the greatest good, and the body's the
greatest evil, does both carnally desire the soul, and carnally
avoid the flesh."

"But the quality of a man's will is of some moment ... And
because none is evil by nature but all by vice, he that lives after
God's love owes his full hate unto the evil; not to hate the man
for his vice, nor to love the vice for the man, but hate the vice
and love the man." XIV, 6

It may come as a surprise to those who have a false view of
Christian asceticism to find that Augustine here goes out of his
way to attack the Stoics for rigorism, and for an over-harsh
attitude to the emotions. According to Cicero the emotions are
classified by them into three constancies and four perturbations.
There are some passions, namely covetousness, exultation, fear
and sadness, which must not be felt by the wise man. Augustine
takes up the position that no passion is evil by nature. Everything depends on its direction by the will. There are some things,
on the other hand, about which we may not feel joy; successful
roguery for example. Again, the Stoics deal too harshly with the
sympathetic emotions. St. Paul counsels us to "weep with them
that weep, and rejoice with them that rejoice." The Christian
life requires a free, full, expansive and social emotional life. A
narrow emotional response is a mark of "great stupidity of body
and barbarism of mind". Augustine goes so far as to say that
"if *apatheia* be an utter abandoning of all mental affections
whatsoever, who will not say that such a stupidity is not worse
than sin?" Those who cultivate impassibility "do rather abjure
true manhood than attain true peace", and there is an asceticism
which is the seed-plot of pride. XIV, 8, 9: IX, 4, 5

Augustine links the criticism of the Stoics into his argument
by describing the condition of our first parents in the earthly XIV, 10-14

paradise, "troubled with no perturbations of mind or sickness of body", and then goes on to describe the fall of man and its effects on man. These sections are important because the effects of the Fall are to be the clue to the interpretation of human history, and what was said about the angelic fall must be recalled here.

God foreknew that man would fall, and what good results He would bring out of his very fall. Yet the fall of man is wrought by his free will and not by any evil in his nature. Like the angels, man fell by pride, tempted thereto by the devil, who envied the uprightness of man. The creature who conveys the temptation is the serpent, "a creature slippery and pliable, wreathed in knots, and fit for his work" (*operi suo congruum*: "like his job"). Augustine likes to emphasize that sin is insinuating, *tortuosus*, productive of circular motions. The temptation of man was to live according to himself, to be his own good, to be as God. "It is good for the soul to be subject, and pernicious for it to leave the Creator's will and to follow its own." Man decides to become self-willed and therefore disobedient. Pride is a "perverse desire of height, in forsaking Him to whom the soul ought solely to cleave ... to make itself seem its own beginning. This is when it likes itself too well, or when it so loves itself that it will abandon that unchangeable good which ought to be more delightful to it than itself." One might say that from this false height man falls from vertigo: his soul goes round and round. The possibility of this fall is rooted in a nature made from nothing, but it takes place from the unnatural viciousness of the will. Man therefore becomes lessened in excellence but not in nature. Man "likes himself as though he were his own light", and then the light is dimmed but the lamp is not destroyed.

Pride, then, dejects, casts down. Augustine is here not speaking only of the original fall, but of a consequence of pride wherever it occurs. Wherever you find pride there you will find an inner misery and dejection, however concealed it may be.

Augustine pauses to ponder on this paradox "that elevation should be below, and dejection aloft". The "dejection" now spoken of is the subjection to higher goods of the humble man. If pride is the root of the vices, humility is the root of the virtues, and therefore a foundation-stone of the City of God. We must therefore be clear about the nature of humility or we shall misconceive the whole superstructure.

If we turn to philosophers like Hobbes or Hume we shall find humility described as a state of abjection, or the possession of an inferiority complex. At the root of their description is their loss of the Christian sense of the hierarchy of being. Augustinian humility is quite simply the sense of belonging to God's universe, and the will to carry out the functions which our place in it entails. In other words, it is the will to true manhood, requiring no undue depreciation of oneself but a just and objective estimate, first of our nature, and next of the peculiar personal capacities of each one of us. It requires an absolute honesty with ourselves, both ontological and moral, and a will to employ our talents to the full. It is therefore the opposite of and the cure for an inferiority complex. It gives a man that sense of security which follows from knowing his true worth. An undue sense of inferiority would in fact be sinful, and a concealed form of pride, or of dejection in the bad sense. If on the one hand humility is a principle of submission, on the other it is a principle of authority. If a man is a ruler or a father it belongs to his place to govern those under his care and a failure to command would be a failure of humility. To be humble is in short *to be in order*, in all senses of the word, and since to be in order is to be capable of action, as opposed to running round in circles, to be humble is to be capable of effective and meaningful action. As Socrates pointed out to Thrasymachus, a man is capable of his work only under the superior law of his work, and for Augustine this law expresses the character of subordination and superordination which God has written across the face of creation. Augustine's "pride", like Plato's "injustice", implies a disordering of the cosmos reaching to the very depths of being. In the spirit in which Socrates tells Callicles that he has forgotten his geometry, Augustine reminds the proud man that stones have weight, something possible only because the world is ordered love.

XIV, 15   Pride, then, is a loss of the power of living ordinately. Because it is the breaking of a due command it is a death, and a principle of death, not because of any quirk of God's but because man has pulled down upon himself the very nature of things. In a passage full of pith and paradox Augustine tells us that man "who might have kept the command and been spiritual in body, became now carnal in mind ... Becoming not as he desired his own master, but falling even from himself, he became his slave that taught him sin, changing his sweet liberty into wretched bondage, being willingly dead in spirit and unwilling to die in the flesh." "What is man's misery other than his own disobedience to himself?"

Man's disobedience to himself is what he merits for disobedience to God. Whereas his body is by nature—that is, in the due order of things—subject to his imperishable mind, it becomes by the inversion of the hierarchy the master of his mind. It introduces the corruptibility of matter into the sphere of the spirit. Death therefore is the failure of ordinate love, and the horror of death is the horror of an alien intrusion from below. This gives us the clue to the connection between lust and death. To lust is to love inordinately, and it brings upon us as a crushing weight things which would be a source of happiness were they used to the glory of God. It *disintegrates* man's nature, tears him to pieces, not only in the sphere of his personal life and experience, but in his communal and historical life. It turns the organic unity of the human race, figured in our descent from one man, into a dust-storm of particles which blow to all the points of the compass.

This puts Augustine in a position to treat of the question ^{XIV, 16 ff} raised at the end of the previous book, how our first parents came "curiously to observe" and cover their privy parts, and how they would have generated children before sinning.

In dealing with this question Augustine has to steer a careful course between the heresy of the Manichees, who regarded bodily intercourse and the generation of children as an evil, and his personal revulsion from his own bodily sins. There are some who see a Manichean mood in the ensuing chapters, but we must remember that Augustine is concentrating here simply upon the ravages of sin, and secondly that the principles which he employs are not Manichean.

Any inordinate desire is a lust, whether it be for power, or money, or women. He is dealing here, however, with what is usually called lust, "the unclean motion of the generative parts". We may add that Chapter 16 is a wonderful example of patristic plain speaking, quite beyond the prurient avoidances of some modern instruction of the faithful. Augustine calls a spade a spade. What constitutes an unclean motion? Not its being a motion. That is, not the posture of the parts for the generative act. What impressed Augustine was the fact that here we have an embarrassing example of involuntary bodily movement. He says that that is why our first parents looked around for a fig-leaf. "The motion will be sometimes importunate against the will, and sometimes immovable when it is desired, and being fervent in the mind, yet will be frozen in the body." Our lust sometimes "wondrously fails" us. In this failure of response, whether positive or negative, in this insubordination of body to mind, Augustine sees the marks of death and disobedience. Observe that Augustine sees the finger of death as much in frigidity as in exaggerated sexuality. The passionate man who said that callousness was worse than sin possibly thought the former the worse. He makes no virtue of frigidity and psychologists might note the connection between pride and sexual impotence. Death has infected marriage itself not because marriage and generation by the communion of bodies is wrong, as the Manichees said, but because bodies have been spoiled by sin.

We must therefore not draw false conclusions from the fact that the sexual act, whether in brothels or the marriage bed, seeks seclusion from a sense of shame. Since the Fall we are no longer naked and unashamed but sew breeches of fig-leaves by seeking physical privacy. The Cynics, who were not "ashamed to make a show of their desire for copulation", were simply being unrealistic. The marriage act in itself is not something to be ashamed of. Being an honest act it "desires to be known", it "desires the sight of the mind". Mentally it is not to be hidden in a corner.

Augustine holds, then, that marriage and sexual reproduction are not consequences of sin. Marriage was instituted by God in paradise, and our first parents were to be one even in the physical sense. The procreation of children belongs "to the glory of marriage and not to the punishment of sin". Bodily fecundity had its role in the first paradise, and that is why the indissolubility of marriage is commanded for the unity of mankind. Given this, neither can we say that marriage has *become* wrong. "But he that says that there should have been neither copulation nor propagation but for sin, what does he else but make sin the origin of the holy number of saints?"

It is, therefore, not the sexual act, and presumably its pleasure, which is evil, but the abuse of it. I am not sure that Augustine is unequivocal with respect to the pleasure, though St. Thomas was later to say that presumably its pleasure was greater in paradise owing to the greater fineness of the human body before sin. Readers may get the impression that by reducing the motions of the sexual organs to the control of reason Augustine would make of sex something so matter-of-fact that its central position in the human make-up would be lost. Certainly some of his examples of control are curious enough. "There are those that can swallow twenty things whole, and pressing their stomach lightly, give you everything up as whole as if they had but put them into a bag".[1] Yet we must not be misled about his main intention. What belongs naturally to the sexual act is good. Lust is inordinate feeling, and inordinate does not primarily mean strong but wrongly directed, untimely and irrational.

Having now "as honestly spoken of these as of any other bodily members", and "investigated the emotions of human generation", Augustine is in a position to speak of the courses run by the two cities. We have seen how they came to earth, we have investigated the principles of human multiplication, and we must ask now what happened next.

[1] Cf. XIV, 26, where Augustine makes a somewhat off-putting comparison between paradisal copulation, and menstruation.

VI

BOOK XV: THE THEOLOGY OF HISTORY

V, II PERHAPS we can best introduce Book XV by going back to Book V. The providence of God, says Augustine, rules all and comprises all. God is the Author of all being, beauty, form, and order, number, weight and measure. "He having left neither heaven, nor earth, nor angel, nor man, no, nor the most base and contemptible creature ... without the true harmony of their parts, and peaceful concord of composition; it is in no way credible that He would leave the kingdoms of men and their bondages and freedoms loose and uncomprised in the laws of His eternal providence."

Human society, then, has its own *physis*, its own intrinsic order and development. It proceeds according to a plan inscribed in it by God, and its movement through history has a meaningful pattern which Augustine is now about to describe. It is sometimes said that Augustine is the first man to have a philosophy of history. In many senses this is not true. If we read the classical historians we shall find many traces of a philosophy of history.[1] It is true, however, that nobody previous to Augustine had looked so deeply into history for the evidences of human nature and human destiny. But precisely on this account his is not a philosophy but a theology of history. Philosophy is something which, in a sense, is possible without revelation. But if the meaning of history is to be found in its providential plan, that is, if it is hidden in the mind of God, it would be for ever closed to us if God did not admit us to His counsels by the reve-

---

[1] See A J. Toynbee, *Greek Historical Thought*, London, 1924

lation which He has given us of His divine life and intentions. That is why Augustine bases his account of the two cities mainly upon Scripture and why he so frequently calls, not upon human wit, but upon God's help to aid him in the writing. One may well question whether a philosophy of history is in fact possible, since the course of history includes revelation, and we cannot hope to understand the latter from the outside. There will always be the danger that we shall endeavour to account for revelation in terms of something else, and conclude, like Comte and Hegel, with a humanist degradation of religion. For Augustine history is essentially religious history. It is the history of the Church, as the creation of God which gives their meaning to human creations. This is an insight which Professor Toynbee has partially recovered, without however grasping the claims of Christianity to be unique. Augustine is trying to give us a glimpse of history *sub specie aeternitatis*. We are to look at it from the point of view of man's eternal end and what we know of that end is what God has told us about it. The effort is philosophical inasmuch as philosophy endeavours to see the world as a comprehensive whole, but the ultimate principle of unity which Augustine employs is theological. The intelligibility achieved is that of his *crede ut intelligas*.

The opening chapters should be carefully read because they XV, 1, 2 contain precious information about Augustine's conception of the two cities. Men are divided into two kinds, those who live according to man and those who live according to God. The life of the latter is possible only by grace. In pursuit of their respective goods these men form two societies which lie inextricably mingled and confused in this world. "These we mystically [*mystice*] call two cities or societies, the one predestined to reign eternally with God, the other condemned to perpetual torment with the devil." I think that Augustine says "mystically" because we are looking at their formation from the point of view of revelation. We can hold that there are two cities only by faith.

The first-begotten member of the earthly city was Cain, the murderer of his brother; the first-begotten member of the heavenly city was Abel, a pilgrim (*peregrinus*) on earth by grace, and by grace a citizen of heaven afterwards. On earth Abel was a "foreigner", a "resident alien". The City of God is foreign or alien to this world. It is recorded of Cain, says Augustine, that he built a city, but Abel built none. "The city of the saints [*sanctorum*, those made just by grace] is above, though it have citizens here upon the earth, wherein it lives as a pilgrim until the time of the kingdom come; and then it gathers all the citizens together in the resurrection of the body."

The problem immediately raises its head, whether all historical communities, or "cities", are the creation of sin. It would seem that the conception of the *civitas terrena* is really a double conception. If we take the example of the earthly Jerusalem, we find that Augustine calls it the "shadow and prophetical image" of the *Civitas Dei*. It is its image, not its finished picture. We find the earthly city in two forms, "the one presenting itself, and the other prefiguring the celestial city, and serving it". On this showing even Jerusalem is terrene. But the next sentence runs: "Our nature, corrupted by sin, produces citizens of earth." It would seem that we must conclude that no city on this earth would be what it is without the Fall, not even the earthly Jerusalem, though it may be called heavenly relative to the Babylons of this world. "A part of the earthly city was made in the image of the heavenly, not signifying itself but another." It is the City of God pilgrim on earth, but still in this sense terrene. Let us observe, to go on with, that the word "terrene" is ambiguous, and be careful to observe in what contexts it is used.

It is as well to remark that nobody who has followed St. Augustine in the various meanings which he gives to the words "heaven" and "earth", for instance, in his expositions of the Lord's Prayer in the homilies on the New Testament, will be sanguine about reducing the conceptions of "heavenly" and "earthly" to any simple formula. And this greatly complicates the question whether by *Civitas Dei* Augustine means the Church. Let us add to this that we find "Church" used in various senses.

If we consult the *Enchiridion*[1] we find a conception of the Church which makes it co-terminous with the *Civitas Dei*. It is "the intelligent creation which constitutes the free Jerusalem". "We are here to understand the whole Church, not that part of it only which wanders as a stranger on the earth ... but that part also which has always from its creation remained steadfast to God in heaven ... This part is made up of the holy angels." In one acceptation, then, the Church includes the holy angels. "I am not even certain upon this point: Whether the sun, and the moon, and all the stars, do not form part of this same society."[2] The Church so understood, angelic and pilgrim, is the society of those who live according to God, and that is the definition of the *Civitas Dei*. Again, in one of his sermons on the Lord's Prayer he says that by heaven we can understand the Church.

If, however, we consider the Church as a mundane institution, that is, as it appears in human experience and in history, we must observe that it contains not only pilgrims but reprobates. Augustine applies the parable of the tares also to the Church. It includes the good and the evil, its wheat is mixed with earth and chaff, it contains wicked clerics. Not only is it pilgrim, then, and to be fully integrated into the *Civitas Dei* only after the resurrection of the body, but it is itself the scene of the confusion of the two cities. It is the widest actual embodiment of the *Civitas Dei* on earth, and may, relatively to other historical groups, be so called; but let us remember here again that our language is ambiguous.

There is therefore no straight answer to the question whether by *Civitas Dei* Augustine means the Church. We are not moving here in a world of clear and distinct ideas but within the

[1] Ch. lvi.   [2] Ch. lviii.

mysteries of iniquity and grace which give rise to two "mystical cities", whose huge contours we can touch only by employing sometimes analogy, allegory, and symbol.

XV, 4, 5 However this may be, Augustine sees in Hebrew history a progressive building of the *Civitas Dei* on earth, and in the history of Rome the rooting on earth of the *civitas terrena*. Chapters 4 and 5 are an application to concrete history of the doctrine of the effects of the fall of man. These chapters are full of meat. Chapter 4 commences: "But the temporal, earthly city (temporal, for when it is condemned to perpetual pains it shall be no more a city) has all its good here upon earth, and therein takes that joy that such an object can afford." Augustine holds that the *Civitas Dei* is finally perfected only after the general resurrection. He here says that the *civitas terrena* will then suffer a final disintegration *qua* city. What holds it together now? Its ability to achieve certain earthly goods which are, in their degree, really goods. Let us remember what is meant by earthly goods. Not simply material goods, because they include goods like domination and rest. What bestows earthiness on them is a quality of the will which seeks them. To seek earthly goods is to seek goods in a certain way, that is, inordinately. Now to exercise an undue preference is to import a principle of disintegration and insubordination into the agent, who becomes infected with the nothingness in created goods; and what is effected is a sort of *peripeteia* or reversal in which the agent gets precisely what he does not want. In Chapter 4 Augustine is applying these principles to Rome. The Roman vice par excellence in his eyes was pride of empire, the *cupido dominandi*. Remember that he was writing after the sack of Rome, and that the first half of the *De Civitate Dei* is largely devoted to a condemnation of Roman vices, failures and disorders culled from the pens of her own historians, particularly Sallust. This chapter contains the essence of his answer to those who attributed the fall of Rome to the Christian faith. Rome has idolized a created good, universal sovereignty, and has both reaped the reward and paid the penalty. "For any part of it [the *civitas terrena*] that wars against another desires to be the world's conqueror, whereas indeed it is vice's slave. And if it conquer, it extols itself and so becomes its own destruction." The sack of Rome, then, is the necessary nemesis of the Roman *cupido dominandi*. "It cannot keep a sovereignty for ever over those whom it has subjugated by conquest."

Augustine is not saying that the Roman *imperium* was not in its way a good.[1] Still less is he condemning the very principle of political authority. The *imperium* was ordained by God as a principle of peace in a sinful world, and as a just reward of patriotism and self-sacrifice. Further, it provided the means for cradling and disseminating the Church. It sought a good but after a human fashion, that is, "according to man", and any good can, as a creature of God, bestow a degree of integrity upon its pursuer. It is man's will that is evil, and not the created good as such. Victory and the resultant peace "are good and God's good gifts". Hence even an evil will can effect a good which God's providence can employ for the building of His city. The pilgrim society can use the goods achieved by Rome with safety and thanksgiving, safety because its will is rightly ordered, and with thanksgiving not to Rome but to God.

Evil in the will, however, is a destructive and divisive principle and Augustine sees it at work throughout history, and throughout Roman history. The first city was founded by a murderer, Cain, and Romulus, the founder of Rome, also killed his brother, though his brother was no better than he. Fratricide presided at the birth of the city. "The strife of Romulus and Remus shows the division of the earthly city in itself, and that of Cain and Abel shows the opposition of the city of men to the City of God." Each city seeks a good, but goods are either

[1] See R. H. Barrow, *Introduction to the City of God*, London, 1950, p. 162 ff. Also Arquillière, *L'Augustinisme politique*, Paris, 1934.

unitive or divisive. "The possession of goodness is not lessened by being shared, nay, it is increased when it has many possessing it in one link and league of charity. Nor shall he ever have it, that will not have it in common; and he that loves a partner in it, shall have it more abundantly."

This deserves a little more comment. In the first place it brings out Augustine's conviction that both in good and in evil man is fundamentally social. He must build a city. The principle of coherence lies in what he seeks. We shall come back to this point later on. Let us simply note here that the distinction between unitive and divisive goods is not the distinction between spiritual and material goods. At first sight, it would seem that it might be. A fine poem, for instance, is not diminished by being heard by many, but if I drink a beer the other man cannot have it. The drink therefore contains a greater potentiality for rousing quarrels. But Augustine is asking us to consider that immaterial goods like glory and sovereignty can arouse the greatest quarrels of all, and that material goods do not necessarily arouse strife. Given human egoism and concupiscence men will fight over, say, a drink. On the other hand a material thing may be the instrument of the highest charity. If two men are both dying of thirst and there is enough water to save only one, then he who freely gives it to the other earns the highest reward of fraternal charity precisely because the good can be used only by one. He has turned it into a *bonum unitivum* by the miracle of grace. It is not a question of *what* we use—that would be Manicheism—but of *how* we use it. The good and the bad use the same things, and outwardly there may not be much difference between them. That is part of the difficulty of sorting out the confusion in this world of the two cities. But the bad man is possessed by his goods, while the good man is a foreigner to them. He administers them for God and not for himself. That is why it is wrong to distinguish the two cities as visible and invisible. In a fundamental way both are invisible. They are kingdoms of wills distinguishable here and now only by God, who is the reader of hearts, and both must use the goods of this world. To see, like Burleigh,[1] an adumbration of the Protestant notion of the invisible Church in St. Augustine is to see in him the relics of his Platonism rather than the new and Christian insight into the sacramentalism of a visible universe in which, by virtue of the Incarnation, things seen and experienced in history can carry the weight of the divine purpose.

[1] R. H. S. Burleigh, *The City of God*, London, Nisbet, 1949.

VII

BOOK XV. 6 TO BOOK XVIII:
THE INTERPRETATION OF HISTORY

WE can pass lightly over the rest of Book XV and over Books XVI, XVII and XVIII. I have found it impossible to interest students in these books, though this may merely be a confession of personal failure. I am trying to get at the mind of St. Augustine. I cannot fully appropriate the mind behind these books, and leave the matter without prejudice to some more sympathetic or intelligent commentator.

In the remarks that follow I have tried briefly to suggest why these books appear to drag, and the essence of the criticism is that Augustine has overdone the allegorical interpretation of Scripture. The criticism is not intended to imply that this interpretation is not valid and indeed indispensable. History is regarded by the Christian as providentially directed, and as an education for the human race in what is to come both in and beyond history. On this view, events in history prefigure and prepare for events which are to come, and achieve their full significance only in the light of what they are symbolizing and leading up to. Thus the choosing of Israel by God to be His people is a first step in the providential action by which the human race is to be redeemed, and Israel seen in the light of the divine design comes to stand for the elect. Again, we find Christ rebuking the Jews for not discerning that He was spoken of by the prophets, that is, for not discerning the spiritual and providential character of their own preparation. St. Paul endeavours to persuade the Jews by showing them that their history has a meaning which they have failed to see. The discernment of hidden meanings in history thus becomes a major and legitimate concern of Christian apologists. Old Testament events are seen as adumbrations of the event of Christ, just as in the New Testament itself the raisings of Lazarus and the widow's son are seen as prefigurations of the Resurrection, and of the raising of mankind from spiritual death.

One of the techniques of doing this is to see the historical event only as the vehicle of an eternal meaning, and then the danger arises of regarding the temporal and local in the event as husks to be stripped off by the spiritual eye. If Eden's fourfold river is seen exclusively as a symbol of the spiritual life there is no reason for digging up Ur of the Chaldees. Augustine learnt his interpretation of Scripture from Ambrose, and it is our contention that the dangers of the method were reinforced in him by his Platonizing. But if we criticize Augustine it is not because he finds types and prefigurations in Scripture, but because he does not balance this by the historian's interest in the factual.

Let us admit that Augustine was no historian. He knew the Old Testament, and he read the classical historians. But he read both to prove a point. In the treatise *On Christian Doctrine* (ii, 28) Augustine tells the Christian why he should study history. In the first place, it helps us to establish a chronology, especially of the events in the life of Christ. In the second place, it helps us to smite the heathen. For instance, when calumniators declared that Christ had learnt something from Plato, Ambrose was able to show that Plato was in Egypt at the same time as Jeremiah, so that it was much more likely that Plato had learnt salutary truths from Jeremiah. Thirdly—and most promising—history has to do with things done, and which cannot be undone, which belong to the "course of time, of which God is the Author and Governor". History must teach us what has happened rather than what we ought to do.

In spite of these last observations of his Augustine lacks the inspiration of the empirical historian: objective truth about *res gestae* for its own sake. That was one of the penalties for the reduction of all the sciences to theology. On the whole, the classical historians on whom he leans cared more about historical truth than Augustine.

Augustine had of course a relatively small body of information at his disposal, but it cannot be argued that he made the best possible use even of that. He is content to ignore nearly everything outside of Roman and Hebrew history, though, for instance, Greek history could have supplied him with a mass of illustrations of his principles.

The root of the trouble is his determination to find in the earthly Jerusalem a symbol and prophetical image of the heavenly. This leads him to concentrate upon the Old Testament for the purpose of finding types, images, foreshadowings, and symbols of things to come. The emphasis may be partly due to the Manichean controversy. The Manichees had seen in the God of the Old Testament an unacceptable figure, and in the Old Testament a despicable book. Augustine had been forced to defend the Old Testament because its God was the God Incarnate of the new dispensation. Had not Christ Himself castigated those who were too blind to see He was the fulfilment of the Prophets?

It would be absurd to deny the strength and validity of this motive. What we are indicating is the shortcomings of its execution. Burleigh puts his finger on the point when he writes: "The Old Testament with its actuality is unintelligible from a Platonic point of view." Had Augustine been truer to his own past and less keen on showing how little the Christian had to learn from Plato he would have been more on his guard against what he actually did learn. The sense of actuality is one of the main casualties of the Platonic metaphysics. For Plato, the real is the eternal, immutable, and self-subsistent, and since actual things do not measure up to this standard, the actual is not the real.

Further, since the real is what is knowable, the actual gains what shreds of intelligibility it has from being referred to the real as a shadow or participation. History loses an intrinsic intelligibility and the door is thrown wide open to the allegorizing mind. The Old Testament is much more truly historical in spirit because it rivets the mind to the significance of the concrete and actual event itself. The difference between Christ and Apollo is that Christ smells of a particular stable, suffered under Pontius Pilate, and was crucified on a historical hummock. It is significant that to the actual coming of Christ Augustine devotes hardly any space at all. The transition from fabulation to fact is more than the method can bear. Having regarded the more factual parts of the Old Testament which will not bear allegorizing as a mere framework for the "significant" parts, the birth in the stable, which is the quintessence of historical fact, and which must support the fable, is itself overwhelmed. One could allegorize Sara but not Cyrinus.[1] It is the Old Testament and not Platonic philosophy which is the charter of empiricism, but it took many centuries for the point to be made clear.

Secular history follows the same search for types. Romulus is the type of a fratricide. The building of the Tower of Babel is "the true type of devilish exaltation". According to Augustine's own theory the cities are confused on earth, but while we hear very little of the workings of the *civitas terrena* among the Hebrews, all that we hear of the operations of the *Civitas Dei* among the Gentiles is a tall story of the Erythrean Sibyl on the basis of which Augustine says "that she seems to me to have been a citizen of the City of God".[2]

It would seem, then, that Augustine has not done the best

---

[1] One of the attractions of St. Luke, and part of his sense of the meaning of the Incarnation, is his accuracy of historical narration. This is hardly likely to be appreciated by a writer who, while willing to utter generalities about the horrors of the Punic Wars, refuses to particularize because "nihil aliud quam scriptores etiam nos erimus historiae".

[2] On the other hand the deception of Esau by Jacob is *non mendacium sed mysterium*!

possible for his own cause. But this must not hide from us the greatness of what he did achieve. Nothing just said touches the validity of the great principles which we have been exploring. Modern Augustinianism still has a great work to do in exploring their empirical bearing. An Augustinianism which has learnt from Marx has a future.

VIII

BOOK XIX: THE SECULAR AND THE CHRISTIAN
CONCEPTIONS OF HAPPINESS

WHATEVER may be the vagaries of Augustine's exposition he preserves a kind of external order in the lay-out of the *De Civitate Dei*: four books on the institution of the cities, four books on their progress, four books on their ends. We have arrived now at the first of the last four. We have finished with human history to date. We are not going to try to predict how the future course of history in time will run, though we can be sure that the great principles extracted from revelation will continue to operate. We are going to speak of last things, of the end or consummation of human life and of the two cities. Augustine believes that history has an end, not only in the sense of a goal, but of a consummation which will not be the annihilation of all that has happened in time but its transformation into a new dimension.[1] Such a consummation belongs to his linear conception of history.

Augustine's jumping-off point is a lost treatise of Marcus XIX, 1-3 Varro, *De Philosophia*, which is a compendium of pagan moral theories with a viewpoint and conclusion of its own. There are various reasons why he should have chosen it. Such summaries were widely used for the conservation and propagation of "culture". Again, Augustine was writing *contra paganos*, and here he had a concentrated target. Further, one suspects that Varro's division of philosophers into two hundred and eighty-eight possible sects both appealed to his sometimes curious ideas

[1] On this point it is worth consulting J. Pieper, *The End of Time*, London, 1954.

about number[1] and order, and gave an immediate impression of
the multiplicity and uncertainty of sin as compared with the
unity and certainty of the teaching of the *Ecclesia Catholica*.

But it must also be pointed out that he starts with Varro because he has certain things in common with Varro and with
pagan philosophy. Augustine was in search of happiness, and
the main interest of classical ethics had been the search for
eudaimonia, for the *vita beata*, for quiet, for peace, for a satisfy-
ing vision, whatever that was placed in, or whatever the means
prescribed. Dr. Nygren, in his *Agape and Eros*, holds it against
Augustine that he infected the Christian idea of love with
Platonic ideas of the ascent of Eros, an infection only dissipated
by the sun of Luther. While any consideration of his general
thesis would be inappropriate here, it remains true that Augustine is himself concerned with the problem of happiness. At the
heart of human life is a desire for happiness, indeed, for an infinite happiness, and man's response to this desire determines
not only the quality of individual life, but the structure and destiny of societies. Everybody loves; *nemo est qui non amet*. Happiness is the satisfaction of love. The tale of the two cities is the
story of their love affairs.

The reader is referred to R. H. Barrow's *Introduction to St.
Augustine* for a careful synopsis and analysis of Varro's position,
and indeed to his analysis of the whole of Book XIX. There
seems no point in doing his work twice. The centre of Augustine's criticism of Varro and the possible positions which he
classifies is that they represent the "daily endeavour of our
worldly philosophers", of those *qui studium sapientiae in saeculi
huius vanitate professi sunt*. They are caught in the vanities of a
secular outlook. They are looking for happiness by their own
powers, in their own strength, and in the things of this world.
Man naturally desires a good the possession of which will be
happiness, but this good is not in himself and *a fortiori* not in

---

[1] For one example among many see *De Doctr. Chr.*, ch. ii, 16.

the things below him. To bring this home Augustine embarks on a description, commencing in Chapter 4, of the miseries of human life. This and the ensuing chapters deal respectively with the following matters: (4) the miseries of man in living with his own mind and body; (5) the drawbacks of the family; (6) the drawbacks of civil rule in a city; (7) the miseries of the world; (8) the drawbacks of the society of men; and finally (9) the disadvantages of having to do with angels. Augustine thus covers comprehensively the whole range of possible associations.

On the whole, Augustine is not to be accused of pessimism. He has told us in the *Confessions* of how he went through the mill himself. He had a sympathetic nature easily moved to tears and sensitive to the *lacrymae rerum*. He has given a realistic account of certain facts, and confronted the philosophers with the question: Here is a set of undeniable facts. How effectively can you claim to have dealt with them?

This chapter commences with his manifesto. "If you ask us XIX, 4 now what the City of God says, first to this question of the supreme good and evil, it will answer at once: Eternal life is the perfection of good, and eternal death the consummation of evil; and the aim of our life must be to avoid the one, and attain the other. Therefore it is written: 'The just shall live by faith'." At one stroke, then, he cuts away the pretensions of philosophy to deal fundamentally with the question of happiness at all. We must live not by philosophy but by faith. But what does faith give us? An absolute certainty about things not seen. The human intellect in its natural employment can have certainty only in proportion to the clarity of its vision. But we cannot see the life beyond this life. Hence the philosophers have stumbled and groped among hypotheses and uncertainties, and have been afraid to commit the solution of something so pressing as the problem of happiness to a realm so fitfully seen. The Scriptures, however, settle the matter with authority and enable us to commence where the philosophers left off.

If the philosophers are condemned to uncertainties about another life, they are also condemned to uncertainties about this, and this poses problems of happiness which are insoluble while we remain among the former uncertainties. Let us look at these uncertainties. We have to live with our bodies and our minds, but with what certain felicities can either provide us? The body is subjected to diseases and deformities. The mind can be twisted by madness, or racked by grief, and nobody is secure against these incursions. It is useless to say, you will be happy if you are sound of mind and body, since happiness then depends on a hypothetical condition beyond our control.

It is useless to say that if we are virtuous we can be happy in spite of these mischances. The Stoics can maintain this position only by denying the reality of evil. But the very virtues themselves bear witness to the pressure of these evils. Temperance presupposes lusts which we must combat, fortitude miseries which must be endured with patience. The lie is given to the Stoic view of evil by their own doctrine of suicide. They commence by saying that evil is only an appearance arising from lack of a rational viewpoint, and then tell us that it is reasonable to kill ourselves when our evils become intolerable. By sheer natural instinct men desire to live. "Mighty are the evils which subdue this natural instinct."

XIX, 5 But let us leave the association of an individual with his own mind and body, and turn to his association with others. Augustine approves the doctrine of the philosophers, such as Plato and Aristotle, that man is by nature a social being. The whole trend of his thought is away from individualist or egoist moral systems. It is not good for man to be alone, but everybody knows that marriage has its inconveniences. Everybody knows, too, that those nearest to us have the greatest power to hurt us, and domestic treachery is one of the worst of ills.

Augustine is not saying that the family is not a good, or that these griefs are inevitable. It is sufficient for his purpose to show that its felicities are uncertain. These things can happen and nobody is secure against them.

Let us turn our attention from the family to the city. We XIX, 6 cannot have civic life without laws and magistrates. But we never have legal justice without miscarriages of justice, without "the ignorance of office, the law's delays". If he who is unjustly condemned suffers, so does the judge. He may pass judgement on the evidence, and in good conscience, because it is his duty, but he remains unenviable.

It would be absurd to conclude from this paragraph, in which Augustine discusses the dilemma of the examiner by torture, that he approved of the extraction of evidence by means of torture. He is simply giving an example of "the sort of thing that happens".

However, Augustine had experience of a much wider world XIX, 7 than the city state. Healey translates: "After the city follows the whole world." The Latin reads *orbis terrae*, and refers to the community of nations established by the rule of Rome, which Augustine here calls "the great Western Babylon". He is not referring to any entity either vague or ideal, but to an actual imperialism. Given the world as it is, people speak different languages and "you may sooner make two brute beasts of two different kinds sociable to one another" than two foreigners of different tongue. "A man had rather be with his own dog than with another man of a strange language."[1] Philosophers may dream of a cosmopolis, but common reason requires common speech. The nearest we have got to that is the Roman attempt to impose Latin everywhere, and whatever good that may have done, this imperialism has meant wars and massacres. He who can look on these without compassion "has lost the natural feeling of a man".

[1] One of the delightful touches in this sombre argument. Augustine was on the side of dogs and small boys against the grown-ups. See *On Christian Doctrine*, ii, 20, where he says that it is delightful (*bellum est*) that the dogs sometimes bite the men who kick and cuff dogs and small boys.

It is interesting to note how often Augustine appeals to natural feeling and compassion. It is a clue to the man. It is of a piece with his criticism of Stoic doctrine as unfeeling, and accounts too for the determined realism of these sections. It is this quality of his which makes the preceding three books seem so out of character.

XIX, 8   This chapter may seem a break in the argument, though in fact it rises out of it. Augustine was a warm-hearted man capable of deep friendships. The *pax Romana* had facilitated travel and therefore separations. The Church had used its ways. Anybody who has priests among his friends knows how they may scatter over the world. An international web of friendships is thus set up which rises superior to the barriers of nations, and constitutes a deeper empire of souls. The chapter has a deeply personal current. Augustine mourns the mischances that may befall mortal men: war, sickness, slavery and the like. The more friends we have the more likely we are to get news of this, and then "who can decipher our sorrows but he that has felt the like?" It is natural for us to enjoy friendships. It is inhuman to forbid all passion, hence it is impossible not to bewail the death of those whom we loved when they were alive.

XIX, 9   This chapter, directed particularly against the Platonists, deals with the widest community of all, the society of angels and men. Earlier in this work we pointed out that if angels and men form one society there must be "friendship" between them. Aristotle has argued that friendship is the cement of the community and Augustine has no quarrel with this opinion. We need not fear that mortal mischances will befall our angelic friends but we are cut off from sociable communication with them because in this life they are not visibly apparent to us. Anybody who believes in a guardian angel, and has longed to consult him, will appreciate why Augustine calls this separation miserable. Again, since the angels belong to a realm which our eyes cannot penetrate, it is easy for us to mistake a demon for a friend. Such, says

Augustine, was the situation of those philosophers who tried to establish means of communication with daemons. We must remember that Augustine lived in a world where magic and spiritualism played a considerable part in the lives of many, and in which a book like *The Golden Ass* had found readers because it reflected the atmosphere of occultism and sensuality, and had a kind of delicious credibility. He concludes by consigning the philosophers to hell. They lived in the devil's monarchy and would share his reward to eternity. As in our own world, Satanism had its greatest hold upon the educated.

It is bound to occur to the reader that there is a great inconsistency between Augustine's condemnation of the Platonists and his own continual Platonizing. One is then tempted to go on to say that much of this Platonizing was "unconscious". But this is always a dangerous course when one has to do with a great intelligence. Augustine's morality with respect to the use of Platonism is quite explicit. He was spoiling the Egyptians. He states his attitude in the *De Doctrina Christiana* (ii, 40): "But if those who are called philosophers, and especially the Platonists, have said anything that is true and in harmony with our faith, we are not only not to fear it, but to claim it for our own use from those who have unlawful possession of it [*iniustis possessoribus*]". Augustine, in this instance, had no scruples about picking fruit in the gardens of the wicked. A man might say and do true things and good, and yet in Augustine's eyes be damnable because *iniustus*.   XIX, 10, 11

Against the miseries of human life, miserable if not always in fact then always in possibility, Augustine sets the certain happiness of eternal life. He brings together the notions of eternity and peace, and places our highest happiness in peace. Complete happiness, peace and eternal life are phrases indicating the same condition, but since the phrase "eternal life" might seem to be ambiguous because it could be taken to apply also to the life

of the everlastingly damned, he prefers to call the end of every
man's desire peace in eternity, or eternity in peace.

XIX, 12, 13 The following chapters are among the greatest passages of the
De Civitate Dei. They are a praise of peace. In view of his recent
treatment of Platonists, there is a certain piquancy in observing
its Platonic overtones, and its debt to the Platonic notion of a
cosmos ruled in all its degrees by justice.

Joy and peace, says Augustine, are desired by all men, and we
can observe the urge towards it even in the activities which seem
most subversive of it. Thus the end of war is peace. "All men
seek peace by war, but none seek war by peace." Some of us
have lived long enough to have heard Mussolini say the opposite, but Augustine's argument still covers the case. The Fascist
is trying to quiet a craving by seeking its object. Ezra Pound's
Bertrans de Born is still seeking a harmony, the "music of the
swords", freedom from "fat boards, bawds, wine and frail
music".

Even a gang of thieves requires peace. They require the concord necessary for carrying out concerted plans, and even the
lone robber enjoys his family life, and enforces law and obedience among its members. Did he rule a city or a nation and were
he called a king instead of a robber, then malicious and covetous
as he still would be, he would still demand order. The striking
force and enjoyment of sin still requires the good which it sub-
verts, feeding on that of which it is a *privatio*.

Let us go further and take from myth a half-man or barbarous
beast like Cacus; still we can say that he wanted to enjoy what
he had, and to preserve the harmony between soul and body
which starvation would destroy. Even an Auschwitz torturer
would thus fall within Augustine's scheme.

If we go down the scale of being we find a social life among the
animals. They help each other in caring for their young, and
even those which are not gregarious live peaceably with their
mates and offspring.

The bonds of human society are so strong that even bad men will fight for the community. They would like, Augustine goes on, to reduce the community beneath their own rule. In this they imitate the hierarchy of beings established by God, but the parody of His ordered peace yet pays a tribute to it. "No vice, however unnatural, can pull nature up by the roots."

If we consider inanimate nature, we shall find that there is as it were an intimation or image of the peace of God to be discerned there too. The chapter ends with a remarkable dissertation on the decomposition of a hanged body, of great philosophic importance. It shows not only that the principle of order and hierarchy, and therefore of love, prevails throughout the universe from the society of intelligences to the realm of chemical phenomena, but that the outraged order will always return. The passage is connected with the passage immediately preceding as follows. The wicked man who sets up as a tyrant has broken with the order of good wills, yet he seeks to establish an order which will enable him to maintain his place. The evil cannot exist without a good, since it is not anything, but a *privatio boni*. The evil man is morally upside down but he falls into an order appropriate to his posture. Let us take an illustration. Hang a man upside down. His agony will mark the disturbance of the natural concord or peace of soul and body. Let the man die. Before his body decomposes it preserves the form and order of the body. It is a piece of peace. Further, by its very weight and dependence it proclaims the laws of the physical order. (We should recall here Augustine's dictum that weight is to the body what love is to the soul.) Let the body decay. Still everything occurs according to law, both with respect to its chemical decomposition, and its transformation into other forms of living matter. God's order receives everything, and this becomes for Augustine a fundamental principle for understanding human society. A society may put itself into an unnatural posture by seeking an inordinate good. But it is bound to exhibit some

degree of order or peace, which, since it contains some traces of
the divine peace, can still be used by men for their eternal peace.[1]
The *pax Romana* may be the peace of imperialist war, but it
provided the Church with the means to spread. It is the peace
of the *civitas terrena*, of a body without life, in which has been
bred the new and supernatural life. But if we call it good we call
it good on account of God and not on account of itself. There
is then a sense in which we can call the *civitas terrena* good, but
a sense which in no way mitigates the sentence of damnation.

XIX, 13   Nature, then, everywhere proclaims the peace of God. We
cannot escape it. It governs and orders all things and sets them
in their due place. We might put it that created peace is the
humility of the universe.

It would not be out of place to mention here that these conceptions are central for the theology as well as for the philosophy
of St. Augustine. They serve as an approach for understanding
both the humility and the humiliation of Christ. We must face
the paradox that if humility is knowing one's place, God is
Humility Himself. His being *is* His knowing of Himself; hence
the Logos by which the world is uttered is archetypal obedience
and humility itself. Christ is God obeying. God as the Creator
of the universe has His place everywhere in that universe so that
the ordination or peace of being is the presence of God in it.
This presence is made manifest in the Incarnation. He came into
His own—the order which He had created by His Word—and
His own received Him not—He was humiliated by His creatures.
Christ, the Word, the humility of God incarnate, restores the
order by reversing the work of death, which only the Creator of

[1] Some of Augustine's most striking expressions of the return of order because
of its all-pervasiveness occur in the *De Musica*. See vi, ch. xi, §30, where we find:
"Qui legem agere noluit, a lege agatur; ita peccantem hominem ordinavit Deus
turpem, non turpiter" and "Quia et in malis operibus nostris Dei opera bona sunt."
In vi, ch. xiv, §46, Augustine says that what corrupts the soul is not the harmony
and beauty of inferior things, but the inharmonious love of them which enslaves
us to them. He comments: "Aliud enim est tenere ordinem, aliud ordine teneri."
See also the striking formula in vi, ch. xiv, §48: "Itaque subditur legibus, qui non
amat leges." See also vi, ch. xvii, §56.

the outraged order could do. Since the principle of order descends *ad infima*, His resurrection is the first-fruits of the resurrection of all nature, since all nature is one order. Christ is the Prince of Peace.

We shall have to return to this later.[1] But it should be mentioned here because there is a temptation, as the unfortunate example of Nygren shows, not to see the full force of Augustine's condemnation of the Platonists, and to emphasize Augustine's doctrine of the ascent of man by love at the expense of his doctrine of the descent of God by love. The latter is primary for Augustine and is implicit in his doctrine of creation. Man can ascend, but only on the stepping-stones of an order of peace provided first by the gratuitous love of God in creating, and secondly by His gratuitous humiliation in the Incarnation. We must not lose our perspectives. Augustine is primarily a theologian and a Christian bishop. He Platonizes, sometimes to the advantage and sometimes to the disadvantage of his thought. But he preserved the faith whole and entire, and it was his faith which carried his philosophy and not his philosophy his faith. When he asserts the primacy of faith he means it, and all attempts to reduce him to his own Platonism must shatter on that rock.

Chapter 13 opens with a great praise of peace.

Peace of the body therefore is an orderly disposal of the parts thereof; peace of the unreasonable soul an ordered control of the appetites thereof; peace of the reasonable soul, a true harmony between knowledge and performance; peace of body and soul a temperate and undiseased habit of nature in the whole creature; peace of mortal man with God is an orderly obedience unto His eternal law performed in faith; peace of man and man is a mutual concord; peace of a family an orderly rule and subjection amongst the parts thereof; peace of a city an orderly command, and obedience amongst the citizens; peace of God's city a most orderly coherence in God and fruition of God; peace of all things is a well-disposed

[1] We shall pick up this theme again in books xxi and xxii.

order. For order is a good disposition of discrepant parts, each in the fittest place.[1]

The chapter continues on a level of sustained brilliance, and is a working out of the theme that evil is *privatio boni*, the full bearing of which theme we now come to see. But there may be some profit in reminding readers, who have seen so much abuse of the idea of order, that order is never for Augustine a tyrannous or external framework by nature. That is the character of inferior orders set up by sin, and even then it is remedial as well as penal, insofar as it keeps us still in contact with God's ordinances. Order is what everything desires by virtue of its nature, and its nature is its resemblance to God. The order or scale of being is a scale of resemblances. It is the spontaneous pattern into which things fall as the spectators of God.

Order and law and due subjection are therefore not things to be suffered but to be enjoyed, and since in a sense a thing *is* its order, the whole scale of nature is primarily there to be enjoyed (*frui*). God made everything for our enjoyment, and it is our tragedy that it is *we* who made it a vale of tears. Beatitude is therefore not to be reached by rejecting this world but by learning to enjoy it. The *civitas terrena* is not this world but the abuse of this world, deriving its substance from the goods which it parasitizes. Augustine therefore ends the chapter with the praise not only of honest social peace, but with gratitude for the material means of life which, used in due manner, contribute not only to human peace, but to eternal life. Thus to eat is not primarily the heavy necessity of an evil body but a praise of God. We can thus assume our food and the means of its production, with all that that implies, into the City of God. The following chapters carry out this theme.

---

[1] Augustine commands a magnificent style, but one strictly subordinate to his purposes. "It is one of the distinctive features of good intellects not to love words, but the truth in words". (*De Doct. Chr.*, iv, 12.) "Whatever may be the majesty of the style, the life of the speaker will count for more in securing the hearer's compliance". (ibid., ch. xxvii.)

The chapter commences with the statement that "all tem- ^{XIX, 14}
poral things are referred by the members thereof [i.e., of the
civitas terrena] unto the benefit of the peace which is resident in
the terrestrial city, and unto the enjoyment of the eternal peace
by the citizens of the heavenly society."

An example may help to define some of the problems involved. Let us suppose that I have an idolatrous love of money.
I decide to make money by cornering the production of oil, and
by persuading everybody to use oil-consuming devices. My
activities have vast ramifications, and bring into being a vast
organization. This organization has a certain intricate order,
and therefore peace, of its own. In that sense it is a good. Oil is
an excellent creature, and some of its excellence infects my
activities. Nevertheless what I have done is to construct a sub-
stantial suburb of hell insofar as my activity is inordinate.
Further, it is bound to lead to social misery, insofar as in my
greed I exploit my labour, or stimulate inordinate desires for
oil-consuming devices. It will be seen, as Eric Gill saw, how
much of our commercial life Augustine would regard as
diabolical.

Now suppose that I am a Christian employed in this organization. Augustine would probably not regard this employment
as unlawful, any more than Christ rebuked the centurion or the
tax-collector for his profession. My employment is my miserable necessity rather than my fault. I should, however, be under
the obligation of using my position well—for instance, by not
stealing from my employer, trying to alleviate unjust working
conditions, devoting my earnings to my family, and so on. In
so doing I should be building the City of God in the devil's city,
the two in this world "lying confusedly together". The seeds of
modern papal directives for Christianizing industry are already
in Augustine.

Let us take another supposition. I am a Christian in honest
possession of vast oil resources. I realize that mankind would

be the better for using more oil in devices which alleviate life. In a spirit of genuine charity I organize the extraction, distribution and fruitful consumption of this oil. I pay a just wage, exploit nobody, make no wars. Would I be building a portal of the City of God? Here I find it very difficult to return Augustine's answer, though how we answer is important for our understanding of the two cities. It is quite likely that he would say that to anybody who viewed the matter realistically the supposition was absurd and Utopian. The premisses are impossible. There is no such thing as a lawful and honest possession in the sense that my title and the institutions which allow me that title are untinged with human sin and misery. I shall be unable to carry out my project without importing, if not the world's sin willingly, then the world's misery unwillingly, into my organization. It would still be part of the *civitas terrena*, though one more easily used for eternal life.

On the other hand, if this is to be Augustine's answer certain inconveniences must follow. It is very hard to see why activity from within an organization to combat the evils within it should better further the City of God than an endeavour to set up an organization which endeavours to obviate those evils. Secondly, there is so clear a difference in quality between the first organization and the second that to apply "terrene" to both is a misuse of language. Thirdly, Augustine's distinction between *uti* and *frui* has some ambiguities.[1] The wicked man *uses* things, that is, bends them to himself; the good man *enjoys* them, that is, refers them to God. Again we are caught in an ambiguity of language. I cannot enjoy some things without a previous process of use. For instance, I may burn a candle to the honour of God, but the whole apparatus of refineries and distribution—things in the sphere of use—must be set up before I can do so. Since they are necessary means to a good end they must themselves be good. Augustine, we hope, cannot intend "pilgrim" to mean one who

[1] See Nygren's discussion in *Agape and Eros*, London 1932-9, vol. ii, pp. 285 ff.

wanders about using the products of the damned as a means to salvation while keeping his own hands clean of the dirty work of worldly organization.

I think we may say (a) that Augustine's argument contains many obscurities which a more empirical habit of mind would have resolved, and that he could not be expected to solve problems which only became urgent when there was a closer connection between Christianity and the economic order; (b) that he had not entirely shaken off Greek ideas of contemplation and banausic work;[1] (c) that in any event there is an enigma or a tension in Christian detachment which perpetually shows up (for instance, the problems sketched turn up again in the early history of the Franciscan Order); (d) that Augustine has caught in an unexampled way the enigmatic character of being as it is presented to a human mind. The coil he gets into about time in the *Confessions* is of a piece with our troubles here. It is only God who can see clearly in these matters. Certainly it is part of Augustine's desire for eternal life that then our thoughts will not slip one into another, but we shall see all in a simple vision. Part of the ambiguity at any rate belongs to the nature of the case.

Let us continue the analysis of the text, however. Man seeks a hierarchy of peaces—of body, of appetite, of soul. But they are subordinate "unto that peace which mortal man has with immortal God, to live in an orderly obedience under His eternal law by faith". Only thus can we have that peace with ourselves which is the true love of ourselves, on which we must model our love of our neighbour when we love him as ourself. From peace

---

[1] See *De Doct. Chr.*, ii, 30, where Augustine speaks about the useful arts whereby we make houses, benches, and dishes; and of medicine, and agriculture and navigation, "which assist God in His operations". "Of these a very superficial and cursory knowledge is to be acquired". See also his treatment of the text "Seek ye first the Kingdom of God" in his treatise on the Sermon on the Mount. It is true that in the treatise on Christian Doctrine he is discussing the knowledge necessary for understanding the Scriptures. But it is also true that the conception of understanding and following the will of God through what a Greek would have deemed banausic work, the conception of what one might call a banausic vocation, seems to be singularly lacking in Augustine.

with God follows peace with our fellows. This peace, however, has a hierarchical structure. Love is not the opposite of authority but its necessary foundation. Augustine thus passes easily from the subject of eternal life to the subject of authority.

He deals first with the authority of the father over his family. It is based on his function of provider. He must see to the "peace" of each member of his family—the peace of health, appeasement of hunger and so on. For this they owe him obedience. Therein lies his authority, and his title is based on the fact that he is the servant of his family.

XIX 15, 16   Men rule with justice over the lower creation. But when it comes to the rule of man over man the question is not so simple. Augustine does not question the natural right to authority of a father. But when it comes to political rule, the natural rule in the order of love is that of a shepherd over his people, as contrasted with that of a king. There is, then, a natural authority, that of the shepherd of his people. But the rule of a king brings in a relation of master and servant and that is unnatural, i.e., it is a consequence of sin. "Sin therefore is the mother of servitude, and the first cause of man's subjection to man".[1] All the empires of the world are therefore empires of sin. It is true that they represent the return of the outraged order of nature, in a manner analogous to that in which the constituents of a dead body settle down to their level. They have therefore a relative goodness which may be well used. It is better to be a slave restrained than a lustful man ungoverned. Indeed the danger to the ruler is the greater.[2] "As humility benefits the servant, so does pride endamage the superior". However, Augustine does not hold that an emperor is *eo ipso* damned. In v, 24 he sketches the character of Christian emperors whom "we call happy here in hope and hereafter in deed". They are happy because they have considered

---

[1] There is a striking passage on the sin of exploiting the souls of others in *De Musica*, vi, ch. xiii, §41. To wish to act on other souls is a manifestation of pride, and a usurpation of God's prerogative.
[2] Cf. iv, 3.

the interests of the governed. But we do not call them happy because their authority is natural, but because, like their good subjects, they make the best of an organization in which sin has implicated them. It would seem that he could with consistency hold that the Roman Empire belongs to the *civitas terrena* and yet that its emperor is a citizen of the *Civitas Dei*. He could hardly do otherwise after the Empire had accepted Christianity. He could further both hold the Empire to be a good, and yet see its downfall as just.

I am not sure whether these observations put me at odds with Barrow or not. He says (pp. 235-6): "St. Augustine therefore attaches high value to the State and interpretations which make him disparage the State seem to be beside the mark." I have not questioned that Augustine set a high value on the State. But I have shown that setting a high value on it is not incompatible with regarding it as part of the *civitas terrena*. After all, we have to set a high value on the devil himself as a nature. But words like "high value" and "disparage" are unscientific here. The question is what is the precise relation of the State to "nature". In Chapter 15 Augustine says "[God] made [man] reasonable, and lord only over the unreasonable, not over man but over beasts." (See further my comment on XI. 16). The verb is *dominari*. But what corresponds to a *rex*, as contrasted with a *pastor*, is a *servus*. This relation, he goes on, is the fruit of sin. Is that a "disparagement" of the State?

Now it is admittedly difficult to square this position with the passage at the end of Chapter 16 where Augustine takes up the Aristotelian position of the relation of the family to the city. "Every family is a part of the city". "The orderly command and obedience in the family have real reference to the orderly rule and subjection in the city." Barrow reasonably enough interprets this as a justification of the city, presumably not only in the sense that the city is a relative good, or the return of outraged order. Given that the treatment of paternal authority follows in Chapter 14 immediately from the statement that the fellowship of a man with others follows directly from his peace with God, Barrow's interpretation has good grounds.

Has Augustine contradicted himself? Let us merely observe that Augustine undoubtedly distinguishes between authority which arises from an ontological relationship—such as the authority of God over man, old over young, man over beast— and "regal rule" arising from man's mistaken valuations. There is then a sense in which a family is natural and an empire not. Perhaps we can get rid of the contradiction by pointing out that for Augustine not every family is a fragment of God's peace. In Chapter 5 he has contrasted the peace of the family with the peace of God. In families too the father may "dominate". Such a family will have real reference to the "orderly rule" of the *civitas terrena*. In any event, to be a member of a Christian family is the best preparation for making the best of the "peace of the earthly city", and in that sense too refers *ad pacem civicam*. Augustine certainly held that Christian families produced the best citizens for Rome.

But it was St. Thomas, not St. Augustine, who restored the authority of the prince to the ontological order.

XIX, 17   The title of Chapter 17 is: "The grounds of the concord and discord between the cities of heaven and earth". The first thing to notice is that there *are* grounds of concord. The cities seem to be presented as black and white, evil and good, damned and saved. However, as so contrasted they are "mystically" taken, invisible. As they exist on earth they must use visible things and build visible institutions. Because visible things are by nature good they import some goodness into the works of the wicked. Again, because the good here on earth share mortal needs and miseries they require similar organizations. Whether a man be good or bad, he must eat, and gardens made by good men and evil may not be very different. A carrot grown by a bad man will nourish a good man, though they nourish themselves to a different effect. There is, then, a certain common ground. "The necessities of this life are common, both to the faithful and the infidel, and to both their families; but the ends of their two usages thereof are far different." Each city seeks its own peace, yet the good can use the "peace", that is, the order and organization, of the wicked. As we have noted before, Augustine usually puts it this way round, leaving us with certain unanswered questions. After all, the good must also grow carrots which the wicked may eat, but what we principally hear about is their pilgrimage among the gardens of the wicked.

However that may be, the two cities do find a *modus communiter vivendi*. The good "willingly obey such laws of the temporal city as order the things pertaining to the sustenance of this mortal life".[1] It is to be noticed that while commentators usually deny that the State for Augustine is, or is a part of, the *civitas terrena*, the argument under consideration has a different tenor. It is the temporal city which is connected with the production of the necessities of this mortal life. Initiatives on the part of the *Civitas Dei* are left unmentioned. Augustine goes on to connect the production of cattle, corn, wine, the conduct of war, navigation, etc., with pagan polytheism, contrasting the latter with the Christian's overriding will to worship one God.

Augustine's emphasis may have been inevitable in a world where Christians were using and inheriting a pagan organization. However, he is pointing to a fact of common experience, that the families of Christians may not live very differently in outward appearance from the families of pagans. Many of their needs are common, so that it is possible for them to live in one commonwealth. Augustine is not counselling the faithful to trek off and found a city of the saints, but rather to make the best of the world as they find it, and to co-operate politically and

---

[1] Cf. *De Doct. Chr.*, ii, 25, where Augustine speaks of dress, ornament, coinage, and weights and measures. "This whole class of human arrangements, which are of convenience for the necessary intercourse of life, the Christian is not by any means to neglect".

economically as best they can, leavening the lump from within. They "observe and respect this temporal peace here on earth, and the coherence of men's wills in honest morality, as far as [they] may with a safe conscience". In fact, they desire it. A Christian, then, is called upon to be a good citizen. Augustine does not use the Pauline text "the powers that be are ordained of God", but we can see how he would understand it.

However, Christians have in a sense two allegiances, and Augustine has a clear vision of the supranational character of the Church. On earth the *Civitas Dei* "increases itself out of all languages, being unconcerned by the different temporal laws that are made; yet not breaking but observing their diversity in divers nations, so long as they tend unto the preservation of earthly peace, and do not oppose the adoration of one God alone." Christians, then, at heart form one community. They are united in the Church. But they are under the obligation to contribute to the national or communal life or culture of the place where they may find themselves. Incidentally, there is in Augustine quite a strong streak of African nationalism.

However, they may not idolize, that is, derive their ultimate values from, or give their unconditional allegiance to, an earthly community. God must be obeyed rather than men. They must be prepared to make a stand on conscience. We must not look in Augustine for a full-blown theory of the relation of Church and State. What he does make clear, however, is that one cannot have the Christian faith without having two allegiances. Rome had combined religious and civic duties so closely that pagans were unable to see that refusal to participate in pagan cults was not treason to the commonwealth. Hence the persecution of the early Christians, who were unwilling to pay religious homage to Rome and to Caesar. Augustine is showing that citizenship is perfectly compatible with the wider allegiance to the *res catholica*. Rome herself had prepared the way for such a state of mind by preserving the structure of the communities in her empire, and yet insisting on the wider allegiance to Rome. She had combined local with a wider patriotism and the Stoics had done much to idealize this conception. Augustine translates this state of affairs to a new level. He is, however, determined to break the connection between economic life and the cult of *daemones* which the philosophers[1] had established and which made co-operation in the work of the world difficult for Christians. It is the Platonists who make good citizenship difficult.

The pilgrim by faith must, then, seek God's peace, use the earthly peace, and include his neighbour in the life of true peace because "he must not be all for himself, but sociable in his life and actions". Augustine therefore includes a positive charity to our pagan neighbours in the life of concord. He had seen the marriage of the two worlds in his parental home, and the influence of his mother on his father.

Chapters 19 and 20 put the finishing touches to the picture of the Christian citizen in Chapter 17. I call the reader's attention to the words "if we are called forth unto a position the law and need of charity binds us to undertake it".

Chapter 18 picks up again the manifesto with which Chapter 4 XIX, 18 commences, and reaffirms the certain basis of faith against the uncertainties of the philosophers. We must remember that soon after his conversion Augustine wrote a treatise *Contra Academicos* in which he had countered a universal doubt with the certainty of his own existence. *Si fallor sum.* Augustine is not opposing, and never does oppose, faith to reason, but is defending the whole range of certainty, natural as well as revealed, against a corrosive doubt which undermines all sides of life. By the "holy, canonical Scriptures we can all walk without doubt". But there are many things which we do not know by faith, and God has not given us our natural capacities in vain. Thus Augustine does not hold that the senses give us only vain or uncertain appearances. We have true knowledge not only by

[1] Healey weakly translates *quosdam suos sapientes* as "some members".

faith, but through the senses, through reason, and by crediting reliable witnesses. We may say, not in Augustine's language, that faith teaches us to be certain of an objective order, and that this certainty overflows to our apprehension of an objective domain of natural things. We can see the foundation of Aquinas' empiricism already being laid by Augustine on the basis of their common faith. In cutting themselves off from the next world the philosophers have cut themselves off also from this. It is the believer who has the best of both worlds, the pilgrim who is most firmly at home. Augustine carries this firm conviction even into the theory of knowledge.

XIX, 21[1] Having now arrived at the conception of a city which really is a city Augustine undertakes to pursue a quarrel with Cicero to which he has adverted in ii, 21.

In Cicero's work *De Re Publica*, Scipio is made to define a commonwealth as the estate of the people, *res populi*. But what is a people? A multitude united in one consent of law and profit: *coetum multitudinis iuris consensu et utilitatis communione sociatum*. However, there is an ambiguity in the word *ius* which Augustine decides to exploit against Cicero. It is the ambiguity of *Gesetzlichkeit* and *Gerechtigkeit*, between legality and righteousness, between law and love. If we take *ius* to mean the body of legal rules recognized and sanctioned by the authority of the State, then Cicero is giving a workable definition. But if we wish to pick a quarrel and insist that *ius* in the definition is to mean righteousness, then we can argue that on Cicero's definition there never was a *Respublica Romana*. Righteousness means primarily giving His due to God. That is the foundation of all hierarchy and of all authority. But the Romans substituted for God a legion of devils, and therefore since there was no righteousness in Rome there was no true *populus* and no true *res publica*. True that there are points in Cicero's argument of which

---

[1] See the analysis of E. Barker in his Introduction to the Everyman edition of the *De Civitate Dei*, pp. xxx ff.

we can approve. He has shown that it is better for the wicked to be under the law than to be left to their wickedness unrestrained. But this is the law of the earthly city, and it presupposes the ordinances of the true God, whose authority is the archetype of righteous rule, and by which alone men can so restrain themselves as to be good citizens.

We have to take in connection with this the conclusion of the XIX, 23 next chapter, where Augustine forcibly states that where God is not recognized as Lord of all "there is no society of man combined in one uniformity of law and profit, and consequently no *populus*, and finally no *res publica* or commonwealth."

The implications of this are very considerable. They lie at the root of the medieval conception of society as a whole, differentiated into civil and ecclesiastical functions, the latter being superior to the former. They account for the claim of the Church to oversee temporal affairs, and for the concept of an established Church. Further, Augustine has made a great contribution to the medieval theory of the subordination of legal rules to justice and to conscience.[1] Aquinas was to hold that a law was not properly speaking a law if it was not a just law, that is, that law was not properly law if it was not binding *in foro conscientiae*. A whole theory of resistance to tyranny was built upon this, so that it is not too much to say that Augustine was opening a way to a conception of political liberty not possible in the pagan world.

We must not press this too far, nor search in Augustine for what is not there. The concord between the two cities spoken of in Chapter 17 reflects the condition of his own world, and it reflects our own better in many respects than the later medieval theory.

Augustine has to come to terms with the world as it is, and XIX, 24 throwing over the definition of Cicero, he substitutes one which

---

[1] "A law which is not just does not seem to me to be a law". (*De Libero Arbitrio*, i, 5, 11.)

is extremely realistic, and perfectly in accord with his general theory. Let us define a *populus* as follows: "A multitude of reasonable creatures conjoined in a general agreement of those things it loves."

We should recollect here the example from the theatre which we used earlier on. The structure of any association corresponds to a good to be obtained and is a response to that good. We desire the good of tennis: we form a tennis club. We desire the good of oil-consuming devices: we get to work accordingly. We desire empire: we build a military state. We desire wealth: we build our institutions accordingly. There is an echo in this of a discussion in Plato's *Laws*.[1] Goods are sought co-operatively since man is naturally social, and the quality of the association derives from the nature of the good and the way in which it is sought. If our *mores* follow upon our *amores*, so do our *respublicae*. Now since goods form a hierarchy, and further are valued according to the good or ill will of man, we arrive at the conception of a hierarchy of possible commonwealths which reminds us strongly of the argument of *Republic*, viii. Whatever the things loved may be, "where there is a multitude of men, conjoined in a common love of what they properly desire, there may fitly be said to be a people. The better that their higher interests are, the better are they themselves; and otherwise the worse. By this definition, Rome had a people, and consequently a commonwealth." There are then degrees of commonwealth-hood corresponding to the degrees of reality. We thus introduce the notion of grades of terrestriality. The Greeks, the Assyrians, the Babylonians on this definition had commonwealths as well as Rome, the "second Babylon". If Rome had the greatest empire it is because she displayed the highest virtues. Yet her virtues (Chapter 25) were rather vices because they were not referred to God. She is not a true commonwealth because *caret iustitiae veritate*.

[1] Bk. i, 628.

Again Augustine's conceptions throw open a vast area for empirical investigation, namely the detailed investigation of the social structures of peoples in relation to the values and preferences by which they live, an investigation which will not be merely positivist but possessed of a criterion of judgement given by the Christian religion. The concept of a sociology which is both empirical and scientific, and at the same time Christian, would thus be given. Augustine's loathing of Babylon blankets this possibility. The Roman commonwealth is directed to its goods by the most vicious devils. What is not of God is of hell.

Book XIX therefore throws light on a much quoted and IV, 4 discussed chapter in Book IV. It is the chapter which commences with the famous words: *Remota itaque iustitia quid sunt regna nisi magna latrocinia? Quia et latrocinia quid sunt nisi parva regna?* "Put justice aside, then, and what are kingdoms but great piracies? For what are pirate organizations if not little kingdoms?" I cannot avoid the conclusion, against Barrow, that since Rome is a *respublica* only upon the realist definition, the Roman *respublica* is to be numbered among the piratical *regna*. If we look at the conclusion of iv, 6 we find Augustine commenting on the actions of Assyria in words like those which elsewhere he uses of Rome. "Now to war against one's neighbours, and to proceed to the hurt of such as hurt not you, for greedy desire of rule and sovereignty, what is this but flat thievery in a greater excess and quantity than usual?" Compare this with what he says of the political behaviour of Rome in xix, 24 and his immediate assimilation there of Rome and Assyria in a common definition.

We cannot conclude from this, however, that he holds out no hope of a Christian commonwealth. Indeed, hope builds it as far as it can be on earth (xix, 20). That which seeks goods in order—that is, seeks the peace of God—would be a commonwealth on the realist definition. Further, and it may seem strangely, it does not preclude an affection for Rome. Here too he has managed to hate the vice and love the nature. Thieves, after all, are not entirely unlovable, and we should not lose sight of Augustine's charity behind his denunciations. There is a touching conclusion to iv, 7, where Augustine refers to the sacking of Rome. Rome is afflicted, he says, rather than submerged in another empire. It has recovered before. It may recover again. *Nec istis temporibus desperandum est.* We must not give up hope yet. "Who knows the will of God herein?"

We shall appreciate better what may seem the curious structure of his mind in this matter if we remember that, for Augustine, every sin is a kind of misdirected search for God. Christ is the Hound of Heaven. In the *Confessions* Augustine tells how, searching for happiness in created things, he was driven on by them until his heart found rest in God. Every man seeks happiness and he seeks it in a good. In a sense, there is no such thing as evil, but only a good wrongly sought. Thus power is not an evil, but an inordinate love of power is. At the heart of everything sought there is a vestige of God, and reminding us as it does of His infinity it arouses an infinite craving. If we do not transcend the creature this craving will manifest itself in an infinite craving for that creature. Thus imperialism arises when, seeking power as an end in itself, we sigh when we have no further worlds to conquer. Loving women without the restraint of higher values we seek to make conquests without end. Seeking money as a final good we seek to extend our financial empire infinitely. Thus we set up, in our misguided love of an infinite peace or good, a series of false infinites or idols which we substitute for the true God. An idol is any creature inordinately pursued, and our very idolatries, our "fornications after strange gods", bear witness to the fact that we are made for God, and shall find eternal peace only in Him. At the heart of every sinner there is, therefore, a desire for God, however perverted. In his sins there is as it were a potentiality of reformation. The eye of charity can see, sometimes in the very magnitude of the sin, the stamp of the Creator on the creature. Some may be the harlot city, the second Babylon, but Augustine is still able to see the good in the Empire, and to thank God for His creature, as in the *Confessions* he can thank God for his youth, in spite of his disordered passions.

The concluding chapters both end the argument against the ^{XIX, 27, 28} philosophers, and anticipate the conclusion of the whole work. The error of the philosophers has been their "secularity". They have failed to look beyond this world. But Augustine has shown that there is no hope in worldly things. Mankind seeks happiness and that happiness is to be found in a highest good, which is eternal life "where God shall be all in all, where eternity shall be firm, and peace most perfect and absolute". (ch. 20.) To enjoy this peace man must be righteous, and righteousness is "to have God his Lord, and himself His subject; his soul master over his body, and his reason over sin", to entreat God for His grace and pardon, and to be grateful for it. The achievement of this end requires the right ordination of our wills, failure in which brings not only mundane misery but a torment which shall be eternal. For better or for worse human life has a dimension beyond the view of the philosophers, and visible only to the eyes of faith.

APPENDIX TO THE ANALYSIS OF
BOOK XIX

READERS who come to St. Augustine from Plato, and have been helped by Plato to understand Augustine, may be surprised by the violence of his attack on the *Platonici*. They should remember that if their education has been exclusively classical, then they are very likely to fail to apprehend the predominance of the Hebreo-Christian outlook in Augustine's composition. Further, the Platonism which Augustine attacked was a neo-Platonism infected with gnostic superstitions, and in the case of Porphyry twisted by impact with something which it could not understand, the Christian faith.

It would be unjust to St. Augustine to Platonize him at the expense of his Christianity. His struggles to free himself from the inadequacies of a medium of philosophic expression which he could not escape, are heroic. M. Gilson, perhaps especially in *L'Être et l'essence*, has brought out the differences between the Christian God and the Platonic One, a difference which Augustine contributed to define. But while the arguments to show that Augustine's conversion was really a conversion to neo-Platonism do not seem to me to hold water, it does seem that he completes rather than contradicts the Platonic tradition, and redeems the very philosophy which he so often attacks. It cannot be said that he attacks its best features.

In the *Confessions* Augustine tells us that what he owed to Platonism was the ability to conceive of an invisible reality. This was a debt which he never repudiated, and a brief estimate of its extent will help in the understanding of Augustine. Without considering the development of these doctrines in neo-Platonism.

which, however, is invaluable in suggesting the correct perspective in which to see Plato, let us look at them as they issue from their source.[1]

The end of the Platonic philosopher is the contemplation of being. This contemplation is not a stare at an alien confrontation, but a *union* through knowledge and love with that which the soul is like. It is not so much an understanding of reality as an instanding in it, an event at the ontological rather than the epistemological level.

The Platonic philosophy requires a certain reality which is proposed to the intelligence, and a certain manner of, and certain requirements for, apprehending it. If this contemplation is a knowing, we must determine what is known, by what in man it is known, and of what nature this knowing is.

Plato holds that the object of the philosophic act is true being, and that that being is entered into by an act of spiritual contact which immediately unites the soul with being. It is a marriage with being. But being is hidden behind the sensible world, while the eye of the soul is obscured by the body, and by our ignorance and wrongdoing. To be united with being, therefore, man must submit himself to a catharsis, both ritual, moral and intellectual. The dialectic of Plato is a process of moral as well as of intellectual ascent and purification.

Plato wishes to transpose both *l'homme moyen sensuel* and his ordinary interests to a new level. The object of our interest must be shifted from the sensible to the supersensible world. The object of true knowledge, knowledge which is *always* true, must be true being, that is, being which is eternal, immutable, and self-identical. The things of sense are in a state of perpetual change. "Being in itself", the object of true knowledge, must be non-

---

[1] See the appreciation of the work and teaching of Socrates in VIII, 3, where he commends the Socratic *ascesis* on the grounds that when it is effected the mind "might tower up to eternity ... and stick firm in contemplation of the nature of that incorporeal and unchangeable and incomprehensible light which contains the causes of all creation."

sensible, visible only to the eye of the soul, seen not by the light of the sun but by an invisible light. The object of *nous*, which is the invisible and essential centre of man, is a self-identical "known". Our intellect apprehends this intelligible "known" only insofar as it purifies itself from contact with the body and with the sensible world. Morality is not a set of conventions but a living response to reality. That is why in the *Phaedo* Plato says that the life of the philosopher is a preparation for death, where death is conceived as the sloughing-off of the body by the soul, as a purification, as the presence of a man to his proper essence. One must therefore live in a certain kind of way in order to be a philosopher, and to contemplate being as it really is. Plato holds that this life is possible only in a city, which must not only be ruled by a philosopher but which must have as its end the formation of contemplatives.

There is therefore a religious element in the philosophy of Plato. The Platonic forms are not gods, and it is very disputable if and in what sense the Form of the Good, or of the Beautiful, or the One, can be called God. Nevertheless, Plato holds that there is something divine in contemplating them. Man divinizes himself by philosophy.

This contemplation of being is wisdom, and philosophy is a love of wisdom. Philosophy is not merely a matter of conceptual clarification and synthesis, though that is part of the ladder of ascent. We are not primarily concerned to construct an inner conceptual coherence, but to in-struct ourselves into Being. The capacity to see this is the measure of our capacity to understand Plato. Man is not the measure. He must measure up to something which he can directly experience as the meat and drink of the soul. He has, if you like, an ontic sense. Spiritually he is touching something, and the absolutely fundamental thing in Plato is this sense of touch. His first principle is being, experienced as a given and indubitable reality.

Here is a primary point of resemblance with St. Augustine,

for whom God is more directly and intimately present than the things of sense, not in theory but in lived experience. It would be a blind reader of Plato who could not discern in him a sense of this Presence as a source of grace, the grace which above all human possibility (*Repub.*, vi) rescues the philosopher from the self-centred life.

The presence of being evokes a love of being, and hence a purification and transposition in the sphere of love. Wisdom is a love of being, and therefore an ordering of our loves for things lacking in being. The highest in the sphere of being is also the highest in the sphere of love, and the ascent of the philosopher is a response to a presence, which leads from the sensual and sensible to love of the invisible. Wisdom brings happiness because it unites us in love to Being. Philosophy is intelligent love.

Further, Plato holds that love is of the like for the like. The ascent of the philosopher is therefore by the ladder of imitation. To know is to assimilate ourselves to reality. It is to *be*, to have the kind of reality which the Forms or Ideas have. In contemplation, then, the soul takes its place actively in the real world. It has the being of a form. It discovers itself as eternal and immutable, immortal and ingenerable. From the fact of philosophic knowledge, the *Phaedo* argues, we can demonstrate the invisibility and the immortality of the soul. The kingly ruler discovers to the citizens their membership of an eternal realm. The end of politics is ecstasy, the *ekstasia* by which the lover of wisdom, in full presence of the Good, the Beautiful, the One, is drawn into an incommunicable communion which is beyond all conception and beyond all speech, and in which *his* happiness is simply Happiness.

Fascinating as may be the question of the relation between Augustine's mysticism and that of Plato, we cannot go into it here. Let us remark, however, that both men knew what it was to embrace invisible being, and to find in wisdom its own validation. We cannot stand outside of it and ask why it is good, without assuming that it is we who are its measure. On the contrary it is what sets everything in its place, as the absolutely final principle of order, number, harmony and measure. And for both men, given that complete happiness is not for this world, there remains the problem of participation in this world, and the problem of the relation of action to contemplation. That is the heart of the question of the relation of the city of this world to the city happy in the real presence of what is.

What they have in common then is a problem of participation arising from the primacy of contemplation. This involves on the one hand certain questions about personal behaviour, and on the other the question of the relation of the sciences and the techniques which are less than wisdom to wisdom. Augustine finds the solution in the subsumption of all the sciences under theology, and Plato in the ordination of all knowledge to dialectic, in the manner represented by the divided line in the *Republic*. Both find the consummation of science in vision, and regard both action and knowledge which is divorced from it as ultimately worthless. This is the problem of the two cities in its ultimate form, since the cities are built by what we are and know.

We shall appreciate Plato's problem better if we take a glance at what he was up against, and if we use some modern examples that may make it more actual for us. We may represent Plato's position thus:

$$\left.\begin{array}{l} \textit{nous} \\ \text{the purified human} \\ \text{essence} \end{array}\right\} \left.\begin{array}{l} \text{contemplates} \\ \text{imitates} \\ \text{is subordinate to} \\ \text{is united to} \end{array}\right\} \text{invisible reality.}$$

This conception of human dignity persisted throughout the Christian Middle Ages. The attack upon it became really serious in late scholasticism, and reached one of its climaxes in the seventeenth century. Descartes brought forward the ideal of a science which was to make us the masters and possessors of nature, thus evoking a very different conception of the relation of mind to reality. Bacon and Hobbes were both concerned to construct a science which would enable us to do rather than to know. We may represent the issue of their conceptions as follows:

Mind is:

(a) capacity for arranging clear and distinct ideas	having discursive, or conceptual, or sense-experimental cognition of arranging or dominating enjoying the fruits of	reality as
(b) or sense impressions		(a) a complexus of natural laws
(c) a capacity for forming concepts or fictions		(b) sense objects
(d) an instrument		(c) sheer individuals
		(d) natural chaos.

The political contrast may be represented at its extreme as follows:

natural community ruling itself by intelligent obedience to contemplated reality } versus { imposition of fiction, by arbitrary will, by and upon natural egoists, to exploit men and nature.

The element of *ascesis* still persisted in the uncontemplative view of reality. Descartes requires us to purge our minds of error, prejudice and confused ideas; Bacon, to get rid of final causes, and of those idols which stand in the way of experimental knowledge. Hobbes and later positivists tell us to clear our minds of belief in all incorporeal and supernatural entities, and confine our attention to sense experience.

There is nothing in this which in principle was not known to Plato except perhaps the extraordinary material success of the programme. It is summed up in what he called sophistry. He regarded its catharsis as perverted. We are emptying out man's essential humanity, which is an immortal capacity for union with the invisible. Man then becomes a mortal being, whose essence will be overcome by death, endeavouring egoistically to dominate a nature which is neutral or meaningless. Meaningless activity then becomes the surrogate for contemplation. Plato knew better than most men the connection between the ontological nihilism of Gorgias, with his "nothing is", and the activism of Callicles.

For Plato too there are two cities, the cities of immortal man concerned with immortal things and of mortal man concerned with mortal things, the cities of the philosopher and of the philodoxer. The contrast takes the form in the *Republic* of the contrast between the waking and the dreaming lives which we may represent as follows:

waking = loving and intelligent union with reality.
dreaming = opinion or belief about sense and change.

The objects of the dream life are those which in different and changing contexts can take contradictory predicates, that is, which are not self-identical.

From this arises a complication in many ways analogous to those of Augustine's position. On the one hand, waking excludes dreaming, the philosopher is not a philodoxer, things of sense are not invisible realities. One chooses a life, and when that life is chosen the other is excluded. Philosophy is not, as Callicles would have it, a parlour accomplishment of educated people. With the excluded life must go the works of the excluded life, and that includes that part of the world's business which is carried on by the "sophistic" mind. The philosopher can have nothing to do with it. Its virtues are his vices. From this arises a dualism of action and contemplation, but it is a dualism which arises out of choice.

On the other hand, however, there is an overriding ontological order which is an order of participations. The visible participates in the invisible, belief participates in contemplation, and Plato has worked out the degrees of participation in considerable detail. The world of belief and of sense is given and to that extent to be accepted. What is a flat incompatibility from the point of view of choice is a graded beauty from the point of view of reality, ontologically justifying those approaches which fall short of unitive contemplation as long as by choice they are not made a surrogate for it.

Implicit in this position is a clear opportunity for validating the sciences of phenomena, and the technical achievements of man. This opportunity Plato does not avail himself of. He continues to regard the conception of sciences of phenomena as self-contradictory, and the return of the wise man to the workaday world as a descent into the cave. In the cave the philosopher is a "pilgrim". We should not on this account, however, underestimate his attempts to do justice to the ontological order, while remaining firm in the order of choice. Only a spiritual evil can corrupt the soul.[1]

A man would choose wrongly in preferring belief to knowledge. Yet in the order of participation belief may be true and right. The world of belief is, in this order, not simply illusion. The philosopher contains the spirited man and the appetitive man in himself. They in turn participate in his wisdom, and their virtue consists in assenting to this. There is an inchoate contemplation in sensual and conceptual apprehension, a position which we can compare with Augustine's position that all men implicitly love God, but have in addition to choose to do so. So seriously does Plato take the value of true belief and of sensible experience that the whole educational system in *Republic*, i-iv, is an education in true belief through physical training and art, which is later to be validated by being scientifically grounded in scientific knowledge consummated by vision. Or to take another aspect, the lower strata in the *Republic*, who do

[1] *Repub.*, 608-11.

not get beyond true belief, are the support of the philsophers, participate vicariously in their contemplation, and rightly claim the service of the guardians, who must be true shepherds of their flock. In the *Laws* Plato insists on the importance of cult and ritual for the populace, not, as is sometimes represented, to turn religion into an *instrumentum regni*, but to offer to the least in the state a participation in the happiness of contemplation. He is endeavouring to make the affairs of the world participate in the good city.

It will be seen, then, that there is considerable resemblance between the positions of Plato and Augustine, arising from Augustine's learning from Plato the possibility of contact with invisible reality. The question arises whether any light is thrown upon the difficulties in Augustine's position by the difficulties in Plato's.

It would be difficult to deny that Plato's assumption of the affairs of the world into the contemplation of the philosopher is not entirely satisfactory, or claim he completely solved the problems of participation. The failure expresses itself, for instance, in his attitude to banausic work, in his frequent contempt for the masses, and in the minimal attention which he pays to their education. The root of this attitude is that he cannot reconcile himself to the sensuality of ordinary men and to his own. The perennial problem is to validate activity and sense experience without falling into activism and sensuality, and to condemn the wrong without, in Nietzsche's phrase, condemning being. It was impossible for Plato to achieve the balance while holding the view that the body is the prison of the soul, and one of the most important approaches to Augustine's conception of the earthly city must be to compare his attitude to the body with Plato's.

Let us first notice that whereas the body of the Platonic man does not participate in his final beatitude, the body of the Christian man does. And it can do so because God created it good. Thus the body and all the activities of the body are re-deemed and validated by the Resurrection. The notion of the body as prison remains in Augustine, however, in another form. It is not, as it is for Plato, the prison of the soul by nature, but only by sin. By sin it has involved the soul in an unnatural realm of corruption and death by which the whole vast realm of human activity which has to do with bodily needs has itself been infected. The need for bodily labour, of eating one's bread in the sweat of one's brow, is the result of the Fall. Given that the whole realm of the sciences of matter and of technics is largely orientated to this need, together with the vast social complexes which they set up, we can see why this whole realm should appear to Augustine to be a prison, and why the empirical sciences enjoy little consideration in his mind. The realm of secular learning is infected with sophistry. It is a sort of rhetoric of being which bars the mind from contemplation, and from this point of view Augustine is more inimical to the world of secular culture than Plato. On the other side, however, the body and bodily labour have a closer connection with the spiritual life for Augustine than for Plato. The body is not by nature a prison, and it, and the things connected with it, have a positive function to play in man's redemption. The world of work is penal and remedial, it is purgative and purificatory, and in that way participates in contemplation in a manner which, given our fallen state, is necessary and intelligible. Through it we enter the Kingdom of God.

But it seems to me to remain true that Augustine inherited from Plato some remains of the prison or cave complex, a certain claustrophobia or asphyxia of being which prevented him from working out the full consequences of the doctrine of the Incarnation, and of the life-giving Body and Bread. It is interesting to observe how little he elaborates the theology of the Eucharist and how often as a consequence a purely "spiritual" interpretation is read into him. The truth of the matter is that he had the sound instinct to keep quiet when he did not have the tools to express himself on matters of radical importance. Aquinas could proceed with this theology because, working with the philosophy of Aristotle and not of Plato, he could conceive of body and soul as a single substance. From this follows a more truly sacramental attitude to the realms of sex, labour and politics, and a more optimistic view about the possibility of assuming them into the life of contemplation. He is more of a Whig than either Plato or Augustine.

The problem of action and contemplation, of the technician and philosopher, is as much our problem as it was Plato's, and it is tempting to pursue the theory of contemplation into the thought of Aquinas. Like Plato, St. Thomas had worldly brothers and came of an active and ruling stock. Like Plato he knew what it was to be tempted on account of his birth and talents to the activistic life. He chased out the world of sophistry with a red-hot brand, and like Plato maintained the primacy of contemplation. It would be *malapropos* to pursue the matter here, however, except to give a hint. For St. Thomas, theology, regarded as a study *divino lumine cognoscibilium*, of things known by the light of a divine illumination, is the summit of human contemplation, a contemplation of which our final beatitude will be a continuation, where its first Principle will reveal Himself to us in full vision. But God is a Creator who knows Himself by the same act by which He does His works. We therefore pose a false question when we ask whether theology is practical or speculative since this either-or is overcome in God, and therefore in ourselves insofar as we are enlightened by Him. In a created universe the "work" and "thought" of God are present without conflict in every creature, and insofar as we share by grace in His life we participate in His simplicity and integrity. We are still in a universe of participation but one in which man, precisely as created, is more closely knit to himself and to the natural world than he could be for either Plato or Augustine

For all of them, however, the contemplative life is consummated in love. *Et propter hoc Gregorius constituit vitam contemplativam in charitate Dei, inquantum aliquis ex dilectione Dei inardescit ad eius pulchritudinem conspiciendam ... ideo vita contemplativa terminatur ad delectationem.*[1] Fundamentally the world is beautiful and therefore lovable because from the Divine Beauty the being of all things is derived.

Festugière remarks: "Plato is a very complex genius. One cannot reduce him to a single image. He enjoyed and despised the things of the world, both at the same time."[2] By selecting the evidence one can construct two incompatible Platos. And the same holds true of Augustine. He knew from experience the abysses and paradoxes of human nature, and one remains truer to his thought by presenting the tensions than by attempting a unification.

[1] *Summa Theol.*, II-II, 180, 1, *ad resp.*: cf. II-II, 180, 7: "Hence Gregory makes the contemplative life consist in loving God inasmuch as anybody who loves God is aflame to see His beauty. Thus the contemplative life is consummated in delight."

[2] *Contemplation et vie contemplative selon Platon*, Paris 1936, 2e ed., p. 449.

IX

BOOK XX: THE LAST THINGS

I HAVE written these pages with a view to the needs principally
of students in a modern university whose interests are mainly
philosophic. A theologian would have written another book and
had in mind, perhaps, another audience. Within the limits of my
métier and my audience I feel neither the capacity nor the obligation to deal with books xx-xxii in the detail with which I
have treated Book XIX.

In a way this is a serious limitation. It does not throw the
emphasis precisely where Augustine would have thrown it. One
reads books on Augustine by classical scholars, by historians,
by political theorists and others and one notices how much has
escaped the net of their preoccupations. We are not big enough
to write about St. Augustine. I have tried to catch something of
the mind of Augustine, and it was the mind of a bishop and a
theologian. Further, the concluding books are intended as a
climax, and as the end which crowns the work. One cannot deal
with the *City of God* without endeavouring to bring out their
significance, and the perspective which they give to the whole
work.

However, what I am attempting is not a learned commentary
on the *De Civitate Dei* but an approach to the work. That is, I
am trying to remove some of the impediments to its appreciation
by cultivated minds; and the worst impediment is the almost
unbelievable ignorance of the Christian universe in the minds of
most of our contemporaries. They do not move naturally within
that universe as, for instance, Shakespeare did. It is useless to go

into detailed arguments about, shall we say, the Resurrection, when it has never really occurred to the person spoken to that it is a matter of practical politics. It seems best therefore to try to get certain broad outlines clear, and to try to show why it should seem reasonable to a man like Augustine to base his life and his outlook upon what to many seem the unrealities of heaven and hell.

We have to remember that that is in part what Augustine himself was trying to do. He was trying to put something across to people, like Varro's philosophers, to whom Augustine's realities were unrealities. He was also trying to confirm and instruct believing Christians in their faith. It is all together in one book but there are two audiences. Sometimes, however, the unbelieving audience had a considerable knowledge of Christian belief upon which Augustine could presume.

Book XX commences, as Augustine so often commences, with the statement that he is going to take his stand on the firm ground of the Holy Scriptures. It must be admitted that Augustine does not by anticipation take the difficulties of the modern atheist at their full weight. He was never himself an atheist, and his objection against the pagans was not that they had no gods but that they had too many. He did not have to persuade his audience that there were daemonic beings, but rather that they had made some more than serious mistakes about them.

Having taken his stand on revealed truths he proceeds to unfold the truths virtually contained in them. In his *Introduction to Saint Augustine*, Barrow,[1] referring to these concluding books, says that here Augustine employed "that ruthless logic which led him to state without any sign of shrinking or horror the harshest of doctrines". "Ruthless" is an emotive term. What must be meant is that Augustine is pursuing an undeviating chain of thought, or that he is consequent in what he holds, or that his

---

[1] "Nunc iam cum misericordibus nostris agendum esse video, et pacifice disputandum!" (xxi, 17.)

premisses lead to the conclusions which he draws. I don't know whether or not it is the harshness of the doctrines which terminates Barrow's commentary at this point. We need not follow Augustine into these books, he says. Why not? The gravamen of Augustine's indictment of the philosophers is that they were content to know nothing of these matters. They were to the Greeks foolishness. Again, if these harsh conclusions are ruthlessly deduced from the premisses then they must be virtually contained in the premisses. If so then the Holy Scriptures must be harsh and capable of producing shrinking or horror. Perhaps they are. Should we therefore shrink in horror from them? But perhaps it is salubrious for us to be harshly spoken to. Consistently with his doctrine of the condition of fallen man, Augustine thinks so. But there is no reason to say that Augustine did not shrink with horror at the thought of the lot of the damned. In fact, so great was his horror that he wrote the *City of God* to pluck as many as possible out of the fire. He did so by trying to show them the ruthless logic of sin. But the logic of sin is God's logic, as he has tried to show. And in showing it, he has endeavoured to prove that its logic derives from the divine love. If we are to boggle at the argument we must start much earlier on. The logic of the argument starts with the being of God, and the centre of Augustine's life was the certainty of the absolute love of God. The cause of the harshness is therefore the divine charity itself, and from this we must conclude that the divine charity is not to be judged by human sentiment.[1] That would be pride. Unless we grasp the central fact that God's condemnation of the wicked, and Augustine's condemnation of the earthly city, are motivated by love, we shall have failed to get our bearings. When Dante inscribed over the gate of hell the words: "Justice moved my High Maker; Divine Power made me, Wisdom Supreme, and Primal Love", he showed that he could under-

---

[1] "Tanto deformius et contra recta Dei verba, quanto sibi videtur sentire clementius." (xxi, 17.)

stand Augustine. What wrote the last books was horror, pity, and hope. It is not remotely probable that the man who on the grounds of his theology accused the Stoics for their lack of lively and sympathetic feelings would by his theology be reduced to an unfeeling logical juggernaut.

I dwell upon this because we have to do here with one of the principal impediments to appreciating the concluding books. It should not be thought that a disbelief in the doctrine of abiding consequences is merely a product of some modern theology, or a sign of the greater refinement of our times. Augustine was well enough acquainted with the "modern mind", since there is a certain repetitiveness about sin. He had heard the difficulty, and replied in these words: "It is in vain, then, that some, indeed very many, make moan over the eternal punishment and perpetual, uninterrmitted torments of the lost, and say they do not believe it shall be so; not, indeed, that they directly oppose themselves to Holy Scripture, but, at the suggestion of their own feelings, they soften down everything that seems hard, and give a milder turn to statements which they think are rather designed to terrify than to be received as literally true."[1]

Augustine holds in common with all orthodox Christians that Christ will come again from heaven to judge both the living and the dead. In that "day" or "time" the tares will be separated from the wheat, and both the good and the wicked will have their reward and their condition eternally fixed. In this life there is much apparent injustice. The good are afflicted, and the wicked are exalted. But when we come to that great judgement, properly called the Day of Judgement, or the Day of the Lord "there we shall not only see all things clearly, but acknowledge all the judgements of God, from the first to the last, to be firmly grounded upon justice". (xx, 2.) In this book Augustine intends, therefore, to set out the Christian belief in the last things.

The Day of Judgement will mark the end of history, and it

[1] *Enchiridion*, cxii.

will be accompanied by the resurrection of the dead. It must be remembered that while there are frequent references in Augustine to the immortality of the soul, that is not nearly so important for him, and indeed for Christianity, as the doctrine of resurrection. Many pagans believed in the immortality of the soul but the doctrine of the resurrection was something peculiarly and centrally Christian. The Apostles were men who had seen and were bearing witness to the resurrected Christ. It is a doctrine continuous with that of the Incarnation, and more remotely with that of creation *ex nihilo*. If matter is not a principle of evil then there is nothing in body which is opposed to the divine goodness. It shares in the divine bounty. For men to possess a body is not an evil but a good. It belongs inseparably to human nature. Christ does not come to save souls but to save men who are wholes of body and soul. The final integrity of man requires that he shall have a body. Otherwise he would not be more but less than man.

Augustine declares that there are two resurrections. Here we must remember what was previously said about the two kinds of death. First, there is the death of the soul which may occur during bodily life by sin. The first resurrection is the regeneration of the soul by the merits of Christ. The second is the resurrection of the body at the Day of Judgement, "sending some into the second death, and others into the life that despises and excludes all death whatsoever". (xx, 6.)

Augustine proceeds to build up the doctrine of the Last Things and of the Resurrection, first, from the New Testament and later from the Old. First, then, he concentrates upon the Revelation of St. John and the teaching of St. Paul. I shall not go into details, since the reader can find a sufficient account in Burleigh's *The City of God*.[1] What we should notice, among other things, is the dramatic character of the religious view of history as compared with the secular. Events take on a new

[1] pp. 139 ff.

dimension; they are filled with new possibilities, and our participation in them is the taking part in a battle, a battle hopeless enough from a merely human point of view, and in which we can survive only by using the weapons of grace. Human history is a sector of the battleground between good and evil, taken not as abstractions but as organizations of good and evil beings. The angels, as both St. John and St. Paul make clear, are deeply involved in the struggle which proceeds in "high places" as well as on earth. They are our allies or our enemies. Thus history is a battle with Satan, and with superhuman powers, fraught with the catastrophes which will precede the day of the Lord.

Further, attention should be drawn to XX, 9 because of its bearing on the question of the relation of the City of God to the Church. Much earlier on we drew attention to the fact that we must be careful to discriminate what Augustine means by "Church" in any particular context. Here he is distinguishing between the Church as it now is, that is, an actual historical organization containing bad men also, and the Church as it shall be hereafter, utterly exempt from evil. Further, he distinguishes between the Kingdom of Christ and the Kingdom of Heaven, and says that the Church now on earth is both *regnum Christi* and *regnum coelorum*. Now, this passage does not permit us to say that Augustine identifies the Church as it now is with the *Civitas Dei*, though we can so identify it[1] if we take "Church" to mean what it means in *Enchiridion*, lvi. Augustine is saying that Christ is here with the Church to the consummation of time. In this sense it is the Kingdom of Christ. It is not yet the glorious Kingdom of Christ which shall be without spot in the eternal peace of God. We can, however, call it *regnum coelorum* insofar as it gathers together here, mixed it is true with the tares, those predestined to reign with Christ in heaven. As the recruiting agency, so to speak, of the City of God we can call it *regnum*

[1] See p. 61.

coelorum, rather in the manner in which a representative of a firm might call himself, for example, "Standard Oil".

The upshot of the whole book can perhaps be most conveniently stated in the words of the *Enchiridion*, which it is convenient to consult frequently because it is Augustine's brief summary of Christian doctrine. Sin divided the two cities. "But when sin had placed a wide gulf between God and the human race, it was expedient that a Mediator, who alone of the human race was born, lived, and died without sin, should reconcile us to God [the first resurrection] and procure even for our bodies a resurrection to eternal life [the second resurrection] in order that the pride of man might be exposed and cured through the humility of God." (ch. 108.) "During the time which intervenes between a man's death and the final resurrection, the soul dwells in a hidden retreat, where it enjoys rest or suffers affliction just in proportion to the merit it has earned by the life which it led on earth." (ch. 109.) "After the resurrection, when the final, universal judgement has been completed, there shall be two kingdoms, each with its own distinct boundaries, the one Christ's, the other the devil's; the one consisting of the good, the other of the bad;—both, however, consisting of angels and men". (ch. 111.)

X

BOOK XXI: THE FATE OF THE LOST

THIS book is likely to be a stumbling block to many because of the meticulous and painstaking manner in which Augustine seeks to prove that the damned will be tormented both in body and in soul, and that that torment will be never-ending. Before we criticize, however, we must try to see the matter as Augustine sees it.

We must remember in the first place that God is not the *cause* of hell. He did not make it, because in fact it is—nothing. Hell is a relapse. It is to be explained by a lapse of the will from rectitude, and "nothing is the cause of the evil will". The tormented city is a multitude of natures which have misused their freedom. They have not forfeited their natures, hence with respect to the natures within it the devil's kingdom is good. In fact it is tormented by its own goodness, that is, by the unavoidable presence of what is absolutely refused. The responsibility for hell is entirely the responsibility of men and of angels. "When we say that men are wilfully unhappy, we do not mean that they wish to be unhappy, but that their will is such that unhappiness is the necessary result."[1]

The chief torment of hell is the absence of God from the wills of its inhabitants. Augustine states this very forcefully in the *Enchiridion*. "To be lost out of the kingdom of God, to be an exile from the City of God, to be alienated from the life of God, to have no share in that great goodness which God hath laid up for them that fear Him ... would be a punishment so great that,

[1] *De Libero Arbitrio*, i, xiv, 30.

supposing it to be eternal, no torments that we know of, continued through as many ages as man's imagination can conceive, could be compared with it."[1] It is impossible to state more clearly that hell is an absence. "Thou hast made us for thyself" says Augustine, so that the torment of hell is the torment of the absence of any end, purpose, or meaning. It is the realm of the meaningless. In a very important sense the fire of hell is the goodness or light of God Himself which scorches because it is refused.[2] It is goodness hated or refused. It is eternity rejected and therefore eternally rejected. Hence if God's goodness and eternity are identical, it is due to the goodness and not to the malice of God that the torment of hell is eternal. Insofar, then, as hell has any cause, that cause is the divine goodness. The magnitude of sin derives from the magnitude of what is rejected, and since what is rejected is infinite, sin is *per se* without exoneration.

Further, if the artificer of hell is created freedom misused we must remember what a compliment to human freedom the doctrine of abiding consequences is. It gives a new and eternal dimension to human responsibility. Animals and plants cannot suffer these torments because they are not good enough. We are, so to speak, burned by the radiance of our own freedom. Only if God had made us worse than He did, that is, less free and intelligent, could the consequences of freedom be mitigated. If we ask for such mitigation it is tantamount to asking God to be less than infinitely generous. God respects the freedom that He has created more than we ourselves do, and the eternity of hell is the last compliment which He can pay it.

If some have read a crushing predestination into the theology of St. Augustine we must call their attention precisely to the doctrine of abiding consequences. We called attention earlier on to Augustine's dispute with Cicero on the compatibility of human

---

[1] *Ench.*, cxii.
[2] "As a sore eye finds the sun sharp". (xxii, 1.)

freedom with the divine foreknowledge. The whole doctrine of what came to be called the efficacy of secondary causes is here at stake. If God knows everything and effects everything, can any created thing do anything? Maimonides reports the opinion of certain Mahomedan theologians who answered, no; and Ockham was to take up a not dissimilar position. That is not Augustine's answer. His answer is that a created cause can really produce an effect which is its own. A created free intelligence is so much the cause or owner of its own acts, so little determined from the outside, that it must claim its acts to eternity. The doctrine of hell is thus the safeguard of a universe in which matches really light pipes, and stones fall because they are heavy. If we are to thank God for a universe which really works then we must thank Him for Hell.

If we ask why God does not put forth His power and annihilate the damned beings the answer must be that He loves them too much. He preserves them in being for the same reason that He preserves the universe in being: because He finds it good. The confidence with which we rest upon God for the perpetuation of the good of being must extend wherever there is being. This confidence is inscribed in the heart of every being as an aspect of the divine image in it, but in the damned it turns to torment by being present without hope.

Further, the doctrine of eternal torment must be taken not in isolation but in the context of the whole of Christian doctrine. If it falls away the glorious things fall away with it, for the Christian universe is a tension of extremes. One can supplement the Christology of the *De Civitate Dei* from elsewhere. Perhaps in particular one should mention the magnificent chapters on the theology of the Redemption in the *De Trinitate*,[1] which form the natural complement to the sections on the fall of man in the *De Civitate Dei*. Perhaps God might have saved man from the consequences of sin without the humiliation of the Cross. But

[1] iv, chs. x, xii, xiii.

He was too humble to do so. We have already indicated in what sense it is true that Christ is the Humility of God. God is humble in the sense that He knows His place, and the act by which He does so is the act by which He keeps all creatures in theirs. In that sense the freedom of man is the humility of God. God respects human freedom by the same act with which He respects Himself, that is, He respects it infinitely. If man is to turn from his sins to God it must not be by any violence laid upon his will but by a free movement or return to the love of God. God presents the lovableness of His creative Word to us in Christ, who overcomes Satan and man's double death by His death, and the torments of His human spirit and flesh upon the cross. The cross is the ultimate persuasion and the only kind of force which God will employ. "And wherein [the devil] received outwardly the power of slaying the Lord in the flesh, therein his inward power, by which he held ourselves, was slain". "And so the devil, in that very death of the flesh, lost man". "The Son of God designed to become our friend in the fellowship of death". In fact, it was the devil who was really crucified. God has gone to incredible extremes, and to the bottom of humiliation, to save man and his freedom. That is the doctrine complementary to the doctrine of the Fall. If man will not respond omnipotence itself can do no more, and hell is the last compliment which God can pay to His own free creation. The pain of hell is the redemptive agony of Christ refused. In a sense, then, it is men who judge themselves. In the suffering of Christ the justice and the mercy of God are both absolute and identical and present us with so majestic a revelation of the divine goodness that Augustine can say of the fall of man: *O felix culpa!*

If these considerations are kept in mind there is no fundamental barrier to the reading of Book XXI, though perhaps a few points could be mentioned in a more desultory way.

Augustine is convinced that the fire of hell must be corporeal as well as spiritual. It is as if the whole creation, in all its range, turns upon the sinner who has outraged its order. Whatever is good, including material creation, is now a curse to him. Further, he holds that this is a consequence of the doctrine of the Resurrection. Man is to be blessed in being, or doomed in being, wholly himself, body and soul. If Christ saves the whole man, body and soul, then man dooms the whole man, body and soul. We may find some of Augustine's physical and chemical analogies rather quaint. But we must remember that they are no more than analogies. The risen body will be different from the mortal body. Of that St. Paul has assured him. "Wherefore though our flesh as now be such that it cannot suffer pain without dying; yet then it shall become of another nature". (xxi, 3.) What this nature shall be can be a matter only of speculation, and all we can say with certainty is that if God can give a body capable of eternal life He can give one capable of eternal suffering. What is the point then of Augustine's incursions into natural history?

Augustine would hold that if God created all beings in His own image then traces of the divine power and mystery must be stamped on every creature, so that the intelligence can find props for what it must hold by faith in the structure of the created world. In his book *Miracles* Mr. C. S. Lewis has followed a method of persuasion not fundamentally different. He finds evidences, hints and intimations of resurrection in nature, and shows that a miracle, in the words of Augustine, *fit non contra naturam, sed contra quam est nota natura*. (xxi, 8.) Miracles have an appositeness to nature, make explicit what is implicit in it: the power of God. Augustine is using the same method, but since his science is not our science the force of his persuasions passes us by more easily. What is instructive is the insight we get into his range of interests. His experiment with the boiled peacock[1] would have pleased Bacon, who caught a fatal illness from refrigerating fowls.

It is usual to accuse Augustine of a hostility to empirical

[1] xxi, 4.

science, but this should be balanced by an examination of his attitude to physical nature. He did a great deal to change the view of nature as an area of demonic infestation to a delight in it as sheer matter of fact. The view of natural laws as customary, the dissociation, for instance, of trees, flowers and crops from priapic contaminations, a sense of the sheer marvellousness of natural events, are in fact Augustine's great contribution to the "scientific attitude". We can compare his attitude here with that of VII. 29. "We worship God, not heaven nor earth", and when we do so, we see the latter as cause, effect, existence, motion, temperature, production, utility, and, in short, as reason open to wonder sees it. Augustine's world is not poisoned by hell. It is truer to say that hell is vindicated by it.

A rather curious line of thought is opened up in Chapter 10 where Augustine raises the question whether the fire of hell, if it be corporeal, can take effect upon the incorporeal devils. Augustine is not prepared, on what he considers adequate scriptural grounds, to dispense the devils from suffering from the same fire as men. "One fire shall torment both men and devils. Christ has spoken it." If the devils are not corporeal this raises some pretty difficulties.

Augustine holds that the angels have airy bodies, on the metaphysical ground that being created they must have a material and mutable substratum. But he does not seem to consider the matter very important for he says: "If any will oppose, and say the devils have no bodies at all, the matter is not great, nor need there be much argument about it." In the *Enchiridion* he is agnostic (ch. 59). He says that certain methods of communication which he has just discussed "seem to imply that angels have not tangible bodies, and make it a very difficult question to solve how the patriarchs washed their feet". He goes on to say that to discuss these matters is a nice intellectual exercise, as long as we don't suppose that we know what we don't. "What is the necessity for affirming, or denying, or defining with accuracy on these subjects, and others like them, when we may without blame be entirely ignorant of them?" Vives comments: "And whereas the Scripture may in some places call them incorporeal, I answer that is in respect of our grosser and more solid bodies, in comparison of which the transparent insensible bodies are ordinarily called incorporeal. Augustine gives the angels most subtle bodies, invisible, active and not passive and such as the devils had ere they fell; but then their bodies were condensate and passive."[1] As we have seen, however, Augustine is easy on the question, perhaps since his argument here can proceed without a definitive solution of the question of the bodies of angels. He has pointed out earlier in the *De Civitate Dei* that what man feels is felt by his soul, which is incorporeal. Pain is a mental not a bodily experience. The pain of the devils is also a spiritual experience though we call it bodily pain. It is called bodily because it is referred to or comes through a body, and the fire of hell may be the means by which this pain is communicated to them as our bodies are the means by which sensations are conveyed to us.

Let us add that Augustine's demonology is a vast subject more prominent in the earlier books than in the later. On the evidence, it is probably correct to say that Augustine attributed aerial bodies to the angels. But the matter is seen in the correct perspective only when we realize that his interest in the matter was primarily theological and not metaphysical. We must remember that his theology of the Redemption is closely connected with his demonology. He repeatedly tells us that Christ cleanses us of the filth imported into human affairs by the devil, and that He does so in His human flesh. It is by the humility of His fleshliness that he slays the "fleshless devil". What he does insist upon is that the devil is fleshless. That is all he requires for his doctrine of the Redemption. But it is quite clear that to establish that the devil is fleshless he does not consider it necessary

[1] And cf. Welldon, vol. ii, p. 636 *n*.1.

to argue that he is incorporeal in the sense of not having even an aerial body. "For these two facts about His incarnation are of no small value, that neither could true divinity be contaminated by the flesh, nor are the devils our betters in having no flesh." (ix, 17.) "But those false and deceitful mediators, the devils ... working strange effects by their aerial bodies, seek to draw us from profit of soul". (ix, 18.)

It is interesting to notice that Augustine's conception of hierarchy appears again in the form of a conception of degrees of beatitude and misery. It is already present in St. Paul with his simile of the varying brightness of stars. In Augustine it rests on the notion of a scale of goods, therefore of *amores* which determine our *mores* and consequently our spiritual status. Speaking of the saints and the damned he says: "Among the former there shall be degrees of happiness, one being more pre-eminently happy than another; and among the latter there shall be degrees of misery, one being more endurably miserable than another".[1] There are as it were layers in both heaven and hell, a conception which was in due course to give rise to the vast structure of the *Divine Comedy*. It is the hierarchical character of the Christian universe which confirms his belief in purgatory, a condition where the punishing fire will be purifying as well as retributive. (xxi, 13, 16.) Consequently he believes in the efficacy of prayers for the dead. (*Ench.*, cx.)

---

[1] *Ench.*, cxi; cf. *De Civ. Dei*, xxii, 30, and *De Musica*, vi, ch. xvii §58: "Rationales et intellectuales numeri ... legem ipsam Dei ... usque ad terrena et inferna iura transmittunt."

XI

BOOK XXII: THE HAPPINESS OF HEAVEN

IN Book XXII Augustine crowns his edifice by discoursing on XXII, 1, 2 the "eternal beatitude of the City of God". God has not designed to pluck chosen souls out of the universe but to recreate the universe, to "create a new heaven and a new earth". Man is, to and in his end, a social being. This end has always been in the foreknowledge of God without any diminution of human freedom. "He did not take away [man's] freedom of choice, foreseeing the good use that He would make of this evil". Augustine insists, here as so frequently, that God achieves His ends not in spite of but through the very evil which He has permitted in the universe, so that even those who oppose His will are in fact contributing to the perfection of His great design. God's will does not change in time but He effects in time what in eternity He has already done. In our last end we shall participate in His eternal action.

At the heart of Augustine's argument is the doctrine of the XXII, 4 resurrection of the body, which he opposes to the argument of the *sapientes mundi*, the philosophers full of secular learning, who argue that such a thing is physically impossible. Here as elsewhere we must observe how deep is Augustine's sense of the wonder of the world in which we live. We take for granted the presence and the operation of a soul in a body. Properly considered, what is occurring there is so marvellous that we can well ask: "Why is it not more strange that a most pure and incorporeal soul should be chained to an earthly body, than that an earthly body should be lifted up to heaven?"

There is a close connection between this doctrine of the resurrection of the body, and Augustine's faith in a new heaven and a new earth. The Redemption is a resurrection of the entire universe. All things re-arise in Christ. This is not a doctrine peculiar to St. Augustine, but rooted in Christian thought and belief. We find it stated succinctly by Aquinas in the last chapter of the *Contra Gentiles*, where he writes:

"After the last judgement has taken place, human nature will have reached its term. But, since all corporeal things were made for man ... it will be fitting that the state of all corporeal creatures should be changed, so as to be in conformity with the state of men, as they then will be. And, seeing that men will then be incorruptible, all corporeal creatures will cease to be in the state of generation and corruption ... 'Time shall be no longer'."

XXII, 5   The testimony of miracles plays a large part in this book, and Augustine here points out that if the resurrection of the body seems incredible, how incredible also is the *fait accompli* of the spread of the Christian Church. The Church, which rests on the witness to the Resurrection, is now spread over the *orbis terrarum*. If the Resurrection be credible, "what fools they are not to believe it! If it be not, how incredible a thing is it, that it should be so generally believed!" Not only is this incredible thing believed, but it was effected by a small band of poor, simple, unlearned men. "That men ignorant in all arts, without rhetoric, logic, or grammar, plain fishers, should be sent by Christ into the sea of this world, only with the nets of faith, and draw such an innumerable multitude of fishes of all sorts, so much the stranger, in that they took many rare philosophers!" Their proofs, he says, lay not in words but in wonders. The Apostles did miracles and in essence these miracles were confirmations of the central miracle of the Resurrection.

XXII, 7, 8;
see also
Book X, chs.
12, 16, 18, 29   Augustine devotes considerable space to the confirmation of the faith by miracles, both in apostolic times and in his own.

The polemic at the commencement of Chapter 8 is very incisive. Augustine was very well acquainted with the kind of person who says: Miracles happened, or may have happened, in apostolic times, but they don't happen now. Augustine declares that their attitude implies that in fact no miracles ever happened at all. He sees that at the root of such a state of mind is a failure of wonder at the universe of our daily lives. Custom blunts its strangeness for us. We have already adverted to this in pointing out, in connection with Book XXI, that in calling our attention to the marvels of chemical and physical phenomena, Augustine is trying to awaken our sense that this universe is the work of God. Miracles are not against nature, but as it were a comment upon it which makes us see it afresh. The universe itself is miraculous, and the fact that man is there at all is a greater miracle than any which may be wrought through his agency. *Creationem rerum visibilium Deus interius operatur*. Man can see only the surface of the continuous miracle of God's creative work, and when a miracle breaks the surface to show us the laws beneath the laws, what is disturbed is human custom rather than God's nature. It goes against what we ordinarily see in nature, rather than against nature.

Augustine, then, is unwilling to accept any *a priori* argument against the possibility of miracles. He will not accept the kind of argument which says that since miracles upset the known laws of nature, those who bear witness to a miracle must be either deceived or lying. He sets a high value upon human testimony, and takes up the attitude that a fact is a fact and if our theories don't fit it we had better change them. We may add that he has good sense on his side insofar as what we may call the humdrum view of nature rests as much upon human testimony as any other.

Now as a matter of fact, he goes on, miracles do happen in our times, and he proceeds to report a number of "modern" miracles, not only well attested by other people but witnessed by himself. There is no need to detail these. It will be sufficient to remark that the miracles are the same kind as those attributed to, say, Blessed Martin de Porres, or the Holy Man of Tours, or the miracles at Lourdes, and are as well attested. If we are persuaded to anything by the latter we shall be persuaded to the same things by the former. A great deal will depend on our antecedent view of nature. If we hold that it is a created nature, then we shall decide the matter on the merits and testimony of each case, and not close the matter before it is opened.

XXII, 9, 10   Augustine then calls in the witness of the martyrs to the miracle of the Resurrection. He is asking how we can refuse to believe the testimony of witnesses whose blood bears witness to the truth which they have seen. Further, the martyrs and the relics of the martyrs have worked wonders by a power which derives from the power of the miracle to which they bear witness. Their miracles are in confirmation of the miracle of the Resurrection, and are done to refer men to God and not to bring any glory to men.[1] We commemorate the martyrs at the altar not on account of themselves but in order to offer to God the honour which is His. "The sacrifice is offered unto God, though it be in memory of them; and he that offers it is a priest of the Lord, and not of theirs; and the offering is the body of the Lord [*corpus est Christi*], which is not offered unto them, because they are that body themselves." Augustine does not here elaborate a theory of the Church as the Mystical Body, or of the new creation as the vestment of Christ, and scholars must decide how much is implicit in what he here says. There seem to be good grounds for saying that he holds that the commemoration of the martyrs rests on the belief that what is offered on the altar is the risen body of Christ, or, at the least, that the themes are inextricably mingled here. The matter is developed further in Chapter 18.[2]

XXII, 11-17, 19-21   These chapters need not be considered in any detail. Augustine is dealing with the host of objections and difficulties which

---

[1] Cf. x, 19 ff.   [2] See Appendix.

are brought forward by those who wish to buttress their incredulity. After the resurrection, will our fingernails grow? Will we have the same sexual organs? Will we still be blondes or brunettes? Will we then have better looks? It is probable that Augustine regarded these matters as irritations to be got rid of, and not as things very germane to his argument. His decisions are ruled by his statement that in fact we do not and cannot really know just what our risen condition will be.

The clue to the placing of these chapters is given in Chapter XXII, 22-4 21. Augustine is now beginning to move towards his final lyric on the joys of heaven, and he asks us to consider what excellent things we already enjoy in this transitory life. Here they are set about with many miseries. If we consider these miseries we shall realize how glorious even this life would be without them, and thus be better persuaded of the wonder of the life to come. In Chapter 22 he gives an account of the calamities of man that oppress any feeling heart. Cicero, he reports, says that no more divine gift could be given to man than the capacity to endure them. The believer, however, has received this gift in Jesus Christ who is therefore called a Saviour.

Chapter 24 is a description of the good things of this life which many commentators for some or other reason seem to find surprising. It is surprising that they should. No man is more likely to speak about the wonders of human nature than the writer of the *Confessions*, nor to appreciate the charm of nature than the saint who held that the vestiges of the divine beauty were imprinted everywhere upon the universe. We find here what we have found before, the sense of the world as a cache of hidden wonders, a miracle in which the resurrection will make explicit that of which we have a foretaste in the natural goods we enjoy. Augustine asks us to consider the wonders of the human make-up, both of body and of intellect, in words from which Hamlet's soliloquy, "What a piece of work is man", might well stem; and goes on to a deep appreciation of natural beauty. His opinion "that the fabric of the bee or ant is more to be wondered at than the whale's" is caught again by Sir Thomas Browne where he writes: "What reason may not go to school to the wisdom of bees, ants, and spiders? ... Ruder heads stand amazed at those prodigious pieces of nature, whales, elephants, dromedaries and camels; these, I confess, are the colossuses and majestick pieces of her hand; but in these narrow engines there is more curious mathematicks; and the civility of these little citizens more neatly sets forth the wisdom of their Maker." Augustine is often accused of being indifferent to physical science, but there is in him much of the vivid love of the world which we find in St. Francis, and the sense of nature not only as something which gives support to faith but which engages the intellect. One catches the echo of this chapter in many bestiaries and herbals.

XXII, 25-8   Augustine returns now to a criticism of the Platonists. If God performs all these natural wonders, "why cannot God raise the flesh unto eternal life? Is it a work unworthy of God? Touching His omnipotence, whereby He works so many wonders, I have said enough already." The reason for this ultimate criticism of Platonism is not hard to find. The clue is in the *Confessions*, where Augustine said that in Platonism he found the doctrine of the Word, but not of the Word made flesh.[1] Platonism lacks the doctrine of the Incarnation and therefore of the Resurrection, and Augustine cannot excuse the blindness of men like Porphyry, who cannot see in the miracle of the Resurrection the completion and not the eversion of their own doctrine. Their major fault is that they cannot appreciate the body, and the significance of the body in the human composition. They think that the return to the body would be a return to the evils of this world. But fundamentally this world is beautiful and full of benefits. The Platonists of his time have failed to appreciate nature, and have therefore failed to appreciate the miracle of

[1] Cf. x, 29.

creation which the Resurrection completes. Their magical practices and cults of the *daemones* are a defilement of nature and
an idolatry of created spirits which poisons both this world and
the other. It is resurrection, not magic, which gives their due
both to nature and to God. Magic is the parody of miracle. The
body of the Lord and the cult of the martyrs is the answer to the
errors of pagan polytheistic daemonism. Retrospectively, thus,
we can better see the bearing of many passages in the first ten
books, where Augustine's argument may have seemed unduly
passionate. The full scope of the issues is now unfolded. The
themes of Book X in particular now come into full perspective,
so that the conclusion of the second half of the work raises to a
higher level the conclusion of the first.

The consummation of human happiness is the vision of God. XXII,29,30
"Truly what manner of action or rather rest and quietness it
shall be, if I say the truth, I know not." It is interesting to
notice, however, how up to the end the faith of Augustine engages his intellect, and how strenuously he endeavours to give
the latter its own proper light. What are we to understand by
seeing, and what share will our resurrected eyes play in it? Shall
we see the material forms of the new heaven and the new earth,
so as to see God present everywhere, and as governing all bodily
things? Here too nature supplies us with an analogy. Even here
when we see men about us, we do not merely believe that they
live but we *see* that they live. Through the body we directly see
the spirit. So in heaven through the body we shall see the
incorporeal God governing all things. "God shall be so known
and conspicuous unto us, that He may be seen by the spirit of
every one of us in every one of us, may be seen in one another,
may be seen in Himself, may be seen in the new heaven and in
the new earth, and in every creature which then shall be; and
may be seen also by the bodies in every body ... Also our
thoughts shall be open to and discovered by one another."

The notion of degrees of beatitude, put into the mouth of

Piccarda by Dante, again appears. "No inferior shall envy his superior ... One shall so have a gift less than another has, that he also has this further gift, that he does not wish to have any more." Where the spirit will be, there shall the body be. We shall enjoy the freedom greater than our earthly freedom in being so near God that we shall be unable to sin. We shall know evil only as God knows it, intellectually and without any admixture of the experience which contaminates. "We shall see that He is God, which we ourselves wanted to be when we fell from Him ... departing from the true God, by whose means we should be gods by participation of Him." The beatific vision then is a dei-fication of man through the humility of God in the Incarnation and not through the pride of man. We shall rest in the peace of the eternal sabbath of God, hymned by Peter Abelard in the *O quanta qualia* which is the purest lyrical expression of the doctrine of Augustine ever attained. *Vera Jerusalem est ille civitas*, and "there we shall rest and see, we shall see and love, we shall love and we shall praise. For what other thing is our end, but to come to that kingdom of which there is no end?"

> Quis Rex, quae curia,
> Quale palatium
> Quae pax, quae requies,
> Quod illud gaudium.

Finally, then: "Let those who think I have performed enough, accepting it with a kind congratulation, give no thanks unto me, but unto the Lord with me."

FINIS

APPENDIX ON THE CHRISTOLOGY
AND ECCLESIOLOGY OF *THE CITY OF GOD*

It is important to see the connection between the Christology
and the demonology of the *City of God*.

A great deal of Augustine's polemic is directed against the
neo-Platonists, and what has to be brought together is Augustine's development of the doctrine of Christ as the Mediator between God and man, and the Platonic conception of the
daemones as mediators between the One and the world.

The universe of neo-Platonism is a universe of descending
participations, going downwards from the One, and pro-
gressively removed from reality the nearer we get to matter and
to multiplicity. Each level mediates between the one above it and
the one below it. It was a conception which worked against
faith in the Incarnation because each level acted as a buffer between the One and the defilement of the One by matter. This
way of looking at things is already present in the *Timaeus*, where
Plato attacks the problem of creation. Plato's first principle does
not soil itself with creation, but effects the work through
subordinate principles. Hence Augustine's insistence that God
is the only Creator and that the angels create nothing. Plato's
conception of the function of daemons is clearly put in the
Symposium (202-3.)[1] "All that is daemonic lies between the
mortal and the immortal. Its functions are to interpret to men
communications from the gods—commandments and favours
from the gods in return for men's attentions—and to convey
prayers and offerings from men to the gods. Being thus between
men and gods the daemon fills up the gap and so acts as a link

[1] Version in Barrow, pp. 210-11, except the last sentence.

joining up the whole. Through it as intermediary pass all forms of divination, all the technique of the priests: sacrifices and rites and spells and divination and sorcery. God does not mix with man. The demonic is the agency through which intercourse and converse takes place between men and gods, whether in waking visions or in dreams—These daemons are many and various and one of them is Love".

"God does not mix with man." That is the doctrine which Augustine knew to be overthrown by the doctrine of the Word made flesh, of incarnate Love, and which accounts for his efforts to establish the goodness of nature, matter and flesh, as the creations of gratuitous divine love. God is mediated to us through matter and the flesh, and before we can appreciate this we must get rid of neo-Platonic notions of mediation.

The Platonists felt the urge to make a bridge, and established not only a metaphysical ladder of being, but a complex of magical, ritual and theurgic practices in order to get into contact with the spiritual realm. Augustine does not doubt either the existence or the efficacy of magical practices. How could he, when the Scriptures bore witness to the operations of Pharaoh's magicians, and when he saw around him the strange goings-on to which missionaries among pagan peoples can in our own day bear witness? He does not doubt that the spirits can manipulate both the appearances of nature, and our minds and senses. In the *De Trinitate* (iv, 2) he writes: "It is easy for the most worthless spirits to do many things by means of aerial bodies, such as to cause wonder to souls which are weighed down by earthly bodies ... Why should it be hard for the devil and his angels to make out of corporeal elements, through their own aerial bodies, things at which the flesh marvels, or even by hidden inspirations to contrive fantastic appearances to the deluding of men's senses, whereby to deceive them, whether awake or asleep, or to drive them into frenzy?"

These devils "of whom no Christian, however ignorant, denies the existence", can play at a kind of false incarnation and false sacramentalism. They can inhabit and be made to inhabit material things like images. They can be contacted by fumigations, herbs, stones, creatures, sounds, words, characters, etc. We can in fact bedevil nature, and for Augustine this is an abominable desecration, by a lust for divine power, of a nature hallowed by the incarnation of our Lord. Magic exhibits the will to exploitation. We may be sure, he argues, that no good angel would so outrage God's order as to suffer to be exploited; and that an evil angel will submit to be exploited, for instance by becoming a familiar, only in order to get us more firmly into its grip.

Against the neo-Platonists and gnostics, then, he sees in the *daemones* nothing in the nature of things, but only fallen angels who have been false to their natures and to God. It is relevant to recall here a patristic notion that the angelic temptation and the occasion of the angelic fall was a preview of the incarnation of the Word, which some then held to be an intolerable slight to the angelic dignity. On this belief the contempt of flesh becomes the origin of all sin, and Manicheism the vilest of heresies. If Augustine be asked what he makes of the scriptural condemnation of "the flesh" he has his answer ready: "The soul, when it lusts after carnal good things, is called the flesh." ("On Faith and the Creed", X.)

The Redemption is represented by Augustine as the overcoming of the realm of diabolical spirits by God who has taken upon Himself our flesh and crucified our sins with it. Mediation is through God incarnate, who by His death in the flesh undoes the work of the false mediators whom we have put between God and ourselves in the belief that God does not mix with man, and who have seduced us to the works of the flesh through our contempt of matter, and our proud admiration and exploitation of spiritual power.

For Augustine the Incarnation and the Resurrection are the

greatest of miracles. His theory of miracles is worked out with specific relation to the Resurrection, his doctrine of which in turn is elaborated in opposition to the neo-Platonic contempt of the flesh. Hence his frequent insistence that the world is not the last pallid remotion from the One, but is itself a miracle.

"But all miracles (done by angels or whatever divine power) confirming the true adoration of one God unto us, we believe truly are done by God's power working in these immortals that love us in true piety. Hear not those that deny that the invisible God works visible miracles. Is not the world a miracle, yet visible, and of His making? Nay, all the miracles done in this world are less than the world itself, the heaven and earth and all therein ... Wherefore God that made heaven and earth—both miracles—scorns not as yet to work miracles in heaven and earth, to draw men's souls, that yet desire visibilities, unto the worship of His invisible being." (x, 12.)

It is because the world is itself a miracle that God does not disdain it, but has condescended to mix with men in the flesh. Pagan miracles are an outrage upon nature. Christian miracles are rather a comment upon it, and refer it to its supernatural source. Augustine holds that miracles are done by angels and by men—for instance, by the martyrs and the relics of the martyrs. But they are done by the power of, and as witness to, the resurrection of the flesh, undoing the death of the flesh worked by the fleshless devil.

It is in this context that Augustine's doctrine of sacrifice and of the Church as a sacrificing body is worked out. The redemption of man is effected by the sacrifice of the incarnate God through the death of His flesh, and by participating sacramentally in His flesh we share in His resurrection.

The devils in their pride demand that sacrifice be made to them. God incarnate made Himself a sacrifice. "Some angels resign all this religious worship to Him, and some would have it to themselves ... If neither of them did any miracles, but the one side demanded sacrifice, and the others said: 'No, God must have all', then ought piety to discern between the pride of the one and the virtue of the other." (x, 16.) Sacrifice is not to be made to the false mediators but to the true Mediator, who, taking our flesh, did not demand sacrifice but became our sacrifice.

"Wherefore the true Mediator, being in the form of a servant, made mediator between God and man, the man Jesus Christ, received sacrifices, as God, with His Father, yet in a servant's form chose rather to be one than to take any, lest some should hereby gather that one might sacrifice unto creatures. By this is He the Priest, Offering and Offerer. The true sacrament whereof is the Church's daily sacrifice: which, being the body of Him, the Head, learns to offer itself by Him." (x, 20.)

"We are one body with Christ, as the Church celebrates in the sacrament of the altar, so well known to the faithful, wherein is shown that in that oblation the Church is offered." (x, 6.)

Augustine's doctrine of the Eucharist and of the Church is thus seen to be worked out in conjunction with his demonology, and cannot be understood apart from it. The Christian sacrifice is rooted in the humiliation of God, which overthrows the pride of the demons, and puts an end to their rites, and to the political and cultural world which they have created.

It is interesting to note that there is in the *City of God* no mention of the mediation of the Mother of God, and no reference to her setting her foot upon the head of the serpent. Lest it be thought that Augustine avoids all reference to the subject, it is right to call attention to a very relevant passage in the *De Agone Christiano*: "But our Lord, Jesus Christ, who came to save men, which includes the saving of both men and women, did not despise men, being made man, nor women, since He was born of a woman. From this arises a great mystery [*sacramentum*] that, as death came to us through a woman, so life was born to us by a woman, in order that by both natures, masculine and feminine, the devil should be overcome and crucified [*victus diabolus cruciaretur*]." In the *De Sancta Virginitate*, Augustine says that through the woman who is the mother of its Head, we are born into the body of the Church.

The cult of the saints and the martyrs, often represented as a survival of pagan polytheism, is presented by Augustine as the answer to pagan diabolism. The martyrs bear witness to the corporate character of the Church and to the miracle of the Resurrection. (xxii, 9, 10.) We can see in proper perspective why Augustine calls the diffusion of the Church miraculous, and uses it to confirm the credibility of the miracle of the Resurrection. We commemorate the martyrs at the altar because they have offered their own flesh and blood in union with, and in the power of, the sacrifice of the Priest whose body is the offering of the Church, whose sacrifice is the act by which the unity of the Church and our union with God is effected. "This mystery, this sacrifice, this priest, this God ... in whom, being now cleansed through faith, and then renewed by sight, and through Him as mediator reconciled to God, we are to cleave to the One, to feast upon the One, to continue one." (*De Trin.*, iv, 7.)

The eucharistic sacrifice is thus the bridge which the neo-Platonists sought through the *daemones*, and the one-ness of the faithful in the body of Christ is the assumption of man into the One from whom the *daemones* separated him. The true City is the City of God in which we co-inhere by sacrifice. (x. 7.) The damned city is the city of magicians and demonolatrous men who place their hope in false mediators who cut man off from God. The Head of the true city is the true Priest who took on our flesh and to whom we shall be finally united in the general resurrection, in which we hope through the sacrifice of the altar "so well known to the faithful".

INDEX